My Adventures With God

With Silver Linings

By Alex Valenzuela

© 2023 Alex Valenzuela. All rights reserved.

No part of this publication may be reproduced, stored in a retrieval system, or transmitted in any form or by any means—electronic, mechanical, photocopy, recording, or any other—except for brief quotations in printed reviews, without the prior permission of the author or publisher.

Scripture quotations marked (AMP) are taken from the Amplified® Bible (AMP), Copyright © 2015 by The Lockman Foundation. Used by permission. lockman.org

Scripture quotations marked (ASV) are taken from the American Standard Version. Public Domain.

Scripture quotations marked (CEB) are taken from the Common English Bible®, CEB® Copyright © 2010, 2011 by Common English Bible.™ Used by permission. All rights reserved worldwide. The "CEB" and "Common English Bible" trademarks are registered in the United States Patent and Trademark Office by Common English Bible. Use of either trademark requires the permission of Common English Bible.

Scripture quotations marked (CEV) are from the Contemporary English Version Copyright © 1991, 1992, 1995 by American Bible Society, Used by Permission.

Scripture quotations marked (ERV) are taken from the Holy Bible: Easy-to-Read Version (ERV), International Edition © 2013, 2016 by Bible League International and used by permission.

Scripture quotations marked (ESV) are taken from the ESV® Bible (The Holy Bible, English Standard Version®).

Copyright © 2001 by Crossway, a publishing ministry of Good News Publishers. Used by permission. All rights reserved.

Scripture quotations marked (GNT) are from the Good News Translation in Today's English Version- Second Edition Copyright © 1992 by American Bible Society. Used by Permission.

Scripture quotations marked (KJV) are taken from the King James Version. Public domain.

Scripture quotations marked (MSG) are taken from THE MESSAGE. Copyright © 1993, 2002, 2018 by Eugene H. Peterson. Used by permission of NavPress. All rights reserved. Represented by Tyndale House Publishers, a Division of Tyndale House Ministries.

Scripture quotations marked (NASB) are taken from the (NASB®) New American Standard Bible®, Copyright © 1960, 1971, 1977, 1995, 2020 by The Lockman Foundation. Used by permission. All rights reserved. lockman.org

Scripture quotations marked (NIrV) are taken from the Holy Bible, New International Reader's Version®, NIrV® Copyright © 1995, 1996, 1998, 2014 by Biblica, Inc.™ Used by permission of Zondervan. All rights reserved worldwide. www.zondervan.com The "NIrV" and "New International Reader's Version" are trademarks registered in the United States Patent and Trademark Office by Biblica, Inc.™

Scripture quotations marked (NIV) are taken from the Holy Bible, New International Version®, NIV®. Copyright © 1973, 1978, 1984, 2011 by Biblica, Inc.® Used by permission of Zondervan. All rights reserved worldwide. www.zondervan.com. The "NIV" and "New International Version" are trademarks registered in the United States Patent and Trademark Office by Biblica, Inc.®

Scripture quotations marked (NKJV) are taken from the New King James Version®. Copyright © 1982 by Thomas Nelson. Used by permission. All rights reserved.

Scripture quotations marked (NLT) are taken from the Holy Bible, New Living Translation. Copyright © 1996, 2004, 2015 by Tyndale House Foundation. Used by permission of Tyndale House Ministries, Carol Stream, Illinois 60188. All rights reserved.

Scripture quotations marked (The Voice) are taken from The Voice™. Copyright © 2012 by Ecclesia Bible Society. Used by permission. All rights reserved.

Scripture quotations marked (TLB) are taken from The Living Bible. Copyright © 1971. Used by permission of Tyndale House Publishers, a Division of Tyndale House Ministries, Carol Stream, Illinois 60188. All rights reserved.

Cover photo and photo on page 155:
https://www.photocase.com/ErinD

ISBN: 9798873165391

Table of Contents

Preface	7
Chapter 1: Salvation is Hard to Explain	9
Chapter 2: Christ's Burning Desire in My Life	15
Chapter 3: He Has a Different Spirit	21
Chapter 4: God Has a Sense of Humor With My Broken Car	27
Chapter 5: The Joy of the Spirit	33
Chapter 6: Four Stages of Salvation	37
Chapter 7: A Ruthless Family	43
Chapter 8: God Healed My Back Injury	49
Chapter 9: Giving by Faith	53
Chapter 10: Joy in the Midst	57
Chapter 11: No Spinal Cord	63
Chapter 12: The Spirit Giveth Life And The Flesh Has To Obey	67
Chapter 13: The Call To Evangelize	73
Chapter 14: Christ Liveth in Me	77
Chapter 15: Believing God's Word During Chaos	83
Chapter 16: No Iris Or Pupil On The Eye	89
Chapter 17: Praying for Rain	93
Chapter 18: Authority Over Demons	101

Chapter 19: Angel of God in the Church Service	107
Chapter 20: Obeyed and Went	113
Chapter 21: Raising The Dead	117
Chapter 22: With God All Things Are Possible	123
Chapter 23: Ending Evangelism and Starting a New Ministry	127
Chapter 24: Call To The Mission Field	131
Chapter 25: Special Love For God's People	137
Chapter 26: Giving Your Best	143
Chapter 27: "Witchcraft" The Necklace Charm	149
Chapter 28: Spiritual Weapons In Mexico	153
Chapter 29: "Witchcraft" and Paralyzed Woman Healed	159
Chapter 30: "Witchcraft" San Luis Potosí, Mexico	165
Chapter 31: "Witchcraft" Spirit of Divination	171
Chapter 32: Equipping God's People	177
Chapter 33: Joy in the Midst of Tragedy	183
Chapter 34: Mercy and Compassion	189
Chapter 35: Being Obedient When God Calls You	193

Preface

If you are starving spiritually and can find nothing to satisfy your hunger, then read this book. This book was written to help encourage, stir, and inspire your steps in faith, so you can receive healing and blessing in your life. I want to pump faith into your soul.

When you read this book please have an open mind and a sincere spirit without putting criticism first. I am sure that you have experienced many of the things I have written. Learn from my experiences and feed, exercise, and develop your faith, and enjoy overcoming the obstacles. Our experiences with the Lord will help you and lead you into the presence of God, and help keep you there. "But blessed are those who trust in the Lord and have made the Lord their hope and confidence" Jeremiah 17:7 (NLT).

The truth is that it is easy to obtain the enjoyment of the Lord in your life. All you have to do is devote yourself to Him. We need to have close contact with the Lord, and be filled with His Spirit. The Lord is more present within you than you may realize. "...because the Kingdom of God is within you" Luke 17:21 (GNT).

My walk with God is like a cloud with a silver lining, because every sad or unpleasant situation has a positive side to it.

Chapter 1
Salvation is Hard to Explain

Acts 4:12 (CEV) says, "Only Jesus has the power to save! His name is the only one in all the world that can save anyone."

A couple of weeks before I went into the military, my brother was sitting in jail awaiting his sentence to go to prison for fourteen counts of "possession of a stolen firearm." A local pastor went to the jail and witnessed to him. He accepted the Lord as his Savior and experienced a wonderful transformation. The judge even noticed it when my brother appeared before him. He was once a violent man, but after he accepted the Lord, he was so gentle and there was no hatred in him. The judge sentenced him to six years in a Bible institute. God is awesome, and I praise and glorify Him. He is the only one who could do something like that.

Every time I went home on vacation from the military, I went out, got drunk with my friends, and didn't get home until the wee hours of the morning. All of a sudden someone would shake me, and when I would open my eyes, I would see my brother looking straight at me, saying "You need Jesus. You remember me for who and what I was?" I would shake my head in agreement, and he would say, "If you could only see what I see, you would know that you need Jesus. It feels so good. I don't know how to give it to you, but I have what you need." My brother and I were never taught anything about God, so it was hard for him to express what he was feeling.

This occurred daily and without change, just like the movie "Groundhog Day." My brother wanted so badly to give me what he had but he didn't know how. 2 Corinthians 5:17 (CEV) says, "Anyone who belongs to Christ is a new person. The past is forgotten, and everything is new."

Our unit and several others were conducting a thirty-day snow package training in Bridgeport, Connecticut. One evening as I was walking to the tent, I saw a young man reading. When he saw me, he put the book away. I went to where he was, uncovered what he was reading, and saw it was the Holy Bible. I said to him, "There is nothing to be ashamed of." Then I explained that my brother had received Christ and I had seen the supernatural power of God in his life.

The day we were leaving, he gave me the address to his parents' house and asked if I would visit them. I visited his parents a few weeks later, and he was there. They lived at a small mission outreach where they showed those who had been saved a better way of life. I visited them every time I went to the Los Angeles area. I never drank in front of them because I had so much respect for them.

There was a young lady named Becky at the mission, and she loved talking to me about God. I loved listening to her because she had the pure love of God in her, as if Jesus was radiating through her. She told me that one day I would be preaching the Word of God, but I would smile and say, "Yeah, right. If you could only see the ugliness inside my heart, you would think differently."

I never felt I was in the same realm as any of them. They were all gentle, loving, caring, and always willing to help. My life was characterized by hate, grief, and turmoil. I would drink and go dancing, trying to fill that gap of love, but the next day my heart still felt empty. I would ask myself why some people get to enjoy a life of love while others live a life of total hate. I would think, *Why did God make me this way to live this kind of life?* I thought it was the hand I was dealt, and I had to play it.

Becky had the love, joy, and peace of God flowing through her, and that's what I wanted. She would say, "If you ever get hold of what I have, you're going to enjoy life. I have so much love, so much joy, and so much peace within me, for God lives in me."

I would say, "How do I get it?"

She would say, "Jesus, He is the answer."

Where do you find Jesus for the answer? I would think. A voice in my mind kept telling me, *If you become like one of them, you can no longer go out and dance, drink, party, or pick up women.* That voice kept telling me I was going to lose everything I enjoyed if I followed their ways.

The devil was dangling enjoyment (sin in the flesh) like a carrot in front of a horse. I would never have missed any of the dancing, drinking, and partying that the devil told me I would lose if I had been saved. It was all a lie because he is the father of all lies.

There was a desire growing within me that wanted that love, joy, and peace that Becky had. I would say, "God, I don't know you, but I want to know you," and then I would ask Him to give me a sign telling me where to go.

One day at the flea market, a man came right at me and introduced himself. I didn't shake his hand; I just walked away. He was lucky I didn't hit him. The lady who was with me said, "You are so stuck up. He was just trying to be friendly."

I walked back to the guy, tapped him on the shoulder, and introduced myself. He was a pastor and invited me to his church. When I visited his church, I met a young man who used to be in a street gang and asked him, "How did you change?"

He said, "God saved me and changed me. Jesus is the answer."

I asked, "How do you find this Jesus?"

He explained that I needed to confess my sins and accept Him as my Savior.

I asked, "How do you do that?"

He said, "It is easy," and he got on his knees and said, "Let us pray." I got on my knees next to him, and he said, "Repeat after me," and I did.

"Lord, I am a sinner and I realize it. Forgive me of all my sins that I have committed, and cleanse me from my sins. I accept Jesus Christ as my personal Savior."

I opened my eyes, and the hate was gone. Instead, I saw everything with so much love, peace, and joy that was beyond this world. I didn't know how to express it. I just knew I had never felt anything like it.

All the young women I saw as my sisters with absolute purity, and the older ones I saw as my mother or my grandmother. I saw the men as my own brothers.

I had such a burning desire to be close to God and for Him to be close to me. I remembered what Becky had said, "If you ever get hold of what I have, you're going to enjoy life. I have so much love, so much joy, and so much peace within me," and I finally understood what she was saying because I have the same feeling she had.

Jesus Christ is living in me. Praise God. God is good to all who call upon Him. Romans 8:16 (NKJV) says, "The Spirit Himself bears witness with our spirit that we are children of God."

After I received Christ as my Savior, I was filled with the Holy Spirit. I finally understood what my brother was trying to say to me. "Remember who and what I was. If you could only see what I see, you would know that you need Jesus. It feels so good. I don't know how to give it to you, but what I have you need."

This was the spiritual transformation he had in Christ. He was talking to me as a baby spirit who had just been reborn. His speech was baba, dada, goo-goo—baby language. He didn't know how to express it.

Jack Coe said in his testimony, "I didn't know what to say, so I ran around the tent, saying 'Hot dog I got it; hot dog I got it.'" 1 Peter 1:8-9 (NIRV) says, "Even though you have not seen him, you love him. Though you do not see him now, you believe in him. You are filled with a glorious joy that can't be put into words. You are receiving the salvation of your souls. This salvation is the final result of your faith."

This glorious feeling of joy is a sensation we cannot express or utter, and we cannot explain it because it is beyond our vocabulary. It is the joy of being engulfed in God's presence. Shekinah Glory ("divine presence").

To God be all the Glory!

Chapter 2
Christ's Burning Desire in My Life

Luke 15:10 (AMP) says, "In the same way, I tell you, there is joy in the presence of the angels of God over one sinner who repents [that is, changes his inner self—his old way of thinking, regrets past sins, lives his life in a way that proves repentance; and seeks God's purpose for his life]."

We are to follow the pattern of Christ. After He committed Himself to serve the living God and was baptized and filled with the Holy Spirit, he preached the Good News. Along the way, He healed the blind and the sick, broke the bonds of the wicked, and freed those who were oppressed. He fed people both physically and spiritually. The Lord was a light that shined wherever He went.

When I was saved and baptized, both in water and by the Holy Spirit, my life changed dramatically. I had that burning desire within me for the Word of God. I spent hours reading the Bible, sleeping only two to four hours a night, and was committed to serving Him with all my soul. The more I searched the scriptures, the more questions I had, so I asked my pastor for the answers. He always told me to just sit in the pew and listen to the sermons and go to Bible college if I desired to do so.

Unfortunately, I never received any answers to my questions. I just don't learn that way. I felt as though the church was trying to put me in a box.

One of the questions I had was why I had a burning desire to witness. One day, as I was reading the Word of God, I found the answer in Acts 1:8 (NIV): "But you will receive power when the Holy Spirit comes on you; and you will be my witnesses in Jerusalem, and in all Judea and Samaria, and to the ends of the earth."

I wasn't in Jerusalem, Judea, or Samaria, but I was in the streets of California. I met some brothers in the Lord who had the same desire I had, and all of us would testify about the Lord, in the streets, at the bus station, in the clubs, and at the laundromats. We couldn't stop telling people what God was doing in our lives.

Acts 5:42 (AMP) says, "And every single day, in the temple [area] and in homes, they did not stop teaching and telling the good news of Jesus as the Christ (the Messiah, the Anointed)."

And Romans 5:5 (NLT) says, Christ is risen, and He is alive. "…For we know how dearly God loves us, because he has given us the Holy Spirit to fill our hearts with his love."

Our witnessing didn't stop there. We started praying for the sick in the name of Jesus, and we saw the power of the Holy Spirit in action as people were healed from whatever sickness they had. Acts 15:12 (AMP) says: "All the people remained silent, and they listened [attentively] to Barnabas and Paul as they described all the signs and wonders (attesting miracles) that God had done through them among the Gentiles."

I was only doing what was written in the scriptures—preaching, teaching, witnessing, testifying, and praying for the sick. I did not want to sit and do nothing. I wanted to follow in Christ's pattern. Mark 16:20 (AMP) says, "And they went out and preached everywhere, while the Lord was working with them and confirming the word by the signs that followed."

My life had been spiritually transformed with a mission to win souls for the kingdom of God and to serve God with all my heart.

Church members started telling me I was wrong and needed training to win souls. I asked them if there was a manual besides the Bible, and they told me I needed to go to Bible college.

I searched the scriptures to see if I was wrong and found the Apostles getting the same pushback in Acts 4:13 (GNT): "The members of the Council were amazed to see how bold Peter and John were and to learn that they were ordinary men of no education. They realized then that they had been companions of Jesus."

They had no Bible education to their name; they were just led by the Holy Spirit, preaching the resurrection of Christ, and telling people to repent and receive Christ as their Savior for the forgiveness of their sins. They were praying in the name of Jesus and the Holy Spirit was doing the healing.

There are two scriptures I call the "before" and "after." The "before" is Luke 24:49 (AMP) where Christ tells His disciples to wait for the promise of the Father, which is the Holy Spirit: "Listen carefully: I am sending the Promise of My Father [the Holy Spirit] upon you; but you are to remain in the city [of Jerusalem] until you are clothed (fully equipped) with power from on high."

The "after" is Acts 2:33 (AMP) when Christ is exalted and at the right hand of the Father and sends us the promise of the Holy Spirit: "Therefore having been exalted to the right hand of God, and having received from the Father the promise of the Holy Spirit, He has poured out this [blessing] which you both see and hear." Being filled with the Holy Spirit is the only "manual" for winning souls to the Lord because He fully equips us with "power from on high." I was only doing and following the examples that the disciples and Christ set for us to do.

I'm not against churches or Bible colleges. But when we have the burning desire of the Holy Spirit within us, it is time to go full speed for the kingdom of God. Bible college takes about four years, and by the time a student graduates, that burning desire might not be there. We can keep it lit only while we are witnessing, testifying, and staying active in the Lord. 2 Timothy 1:6 (NLT) says, "This is why I remind you to fan into flames the spiritual gift God gave you when I laid my hands on you."

One year after my conversion, the Lord told me to leave California and go to San Antonio, Texas. Sometimes God's direction doesn't make sense to us. This was a scary move to me because I didn't know anyone there. While in San Antonio I got lost and asked a guy for directions, and I discovered that he had the same burning desire for God that I did. Our souls were mended together as though we were one in the Lord. Every day we would meet together and go to the streets to witness and testify. We were doing what Matthew 28:18-20 (KJV) told us to do:

> And Jesus came and spake unto them, saying, All power is given unto me in heaven and in earth. Go ye therefore, and teach all nations, baptizing them in the name of the Father, and of the Son, and of the Holy Ghost: Teaching them to observe all things whatsoever I have commanded you: and, lo, I am with you always, even unto the end of the world. Amen.

Ephesians 1:13 (GNT) adds, "...You believed in Christ, and God put his stamp of ownership on you by giving you the Holy Spirit he had promised."

If we follow the pattern that Christ laid out for us, if we are filled with the Holy Spirit, and if we are staying active in witnessing and testifying, we will see the signs and wonders in our lives.

To God be all the Glory!

Chapter 3
He Has a Different Spirit

When I read the story of Caleb, I see that God says he has a different spirit. Numbers 14:24 (MSG) says, "But my servant Caleb—this is a different story. He has a different spirit; he follows me passionately...."

The same scripture in the CEV is, "But my servant Caleb isn't like the others. So because he has faith in me...."

The Voice translation renders it as, "For Caleb, though, it's a different matter. He's distinct from the others by having a different spirit and has followed My lead wholeheartedly...."

I would paraphrase it this way: "But my servant, Caleb, this is a different matter, and a different story; he is not like the others. He is distinct from the others by having a different spirit because he has faith in me, and he follows me passionately and wholeheartedly."

We need to have the spirit of Joshua and Caleb in Numbers 14:9 (CEV): "The Lord is on our side, and they won't stand a chance against us." They weren't looking at the giants in front of them. They were looking at the situation through the eyes of a child by trusting God as their Father: "My daddy is stronger than yours; my daddy is faster than yours; my daddy is greater than yours; my daddy, who is my God, lives within me."

For the first three months after I accepted the Lord as my Savior, I felt as if I was being attacked from all sides. I was living off base, but because of an error, I didn't get paid for three months. Someone in HR would fix it, and another person in HR would reject it.

I borrowed money from all my Christian friends and eventually exhausted everyone I knew, especially since no one makes much money in the military. At that point, I just felt lost; I didn't know what to do.

When I read 2 Kings 4:1-7, I like to think the widow borrowed money from all her neighbors, friends, family, and anyone else who would listen to her. After she exhausted everyone, she probably felt alone and helpless and then turned to the man of God, who told her to borrow empty bottles from the same people she tried to borrow money from.

All those people were now willing to give her all the empty bottles she wanted. Then the man of God instructed her, "Once you have the bottles, close the door and start filling them up with the little oil that you have." She trusted the man of God at his word, and God did the miracle.

One day the man who was giving me a ride to work started hounding me for gas money. When I didn't have any, he quit taking me to work. So, I had to get up an hour earlier to hitchhike. One day someone saw me hitchhiking and picked me up. We were rear ended, and I suffered a back injury. They took me to the hospital, and the doctor told me, "I know exactly where your pain is."

"Yeah, right," I said.

He started pressing his hand exactly where I was feeling the pain. I looked at him and asked, "How do you know that?"

He replied, "Your back is swollen."

The military didn't wait for me to get better and started the process of discharging me. I fought to stay in, but with no success.

The unit I was in went overseas, so I was transferred to a new unit where I met some brothers in the Lord, and they had a burning desire to win souls for the kingdom of God, like Jeremiah 20:9 (GNT) says, "…then your message is like a fire burning deep within me…." So, we would get together and pray and study the Word.

Before long, they started taking me to witness in the streets, the bus station, the clubs, and the laundromats, and we testified for the Lord. This was the burning desire within us; we couldn't stop telling people about God and what He was doing in our lives.

The Apostle Paul also had a burning desire to win souls for the Lord. He says in Acts 20:24 (AMP):

> But I do not consider my life as something of value or dear to me, so that I may [with joy] finish my course and the ministry which I received from the Lord Jesus, to testify faithfully of the good news of God's [precious, undeserved] grace [which makes us free of the guilt of sin and grants us eternal life].

All I wanted was to testify faithfully of the Good News of God. One of my cousins told me, "I don't hate you; it is just hard to talk to you because you always talk about the Lord." People usually love to spend hours talking about their favorite topic, whether it be sports, cooking, or politics. So, why couldn't I talk about what God was doing in my life? Colossians 3:16 (NASB) instructs us to "Let the word of Christ richly dwell within you, with all wisdom teaching and admonishing one another with psalms, hymns, and spiritual songs, singing with thankfulness in your hearts to God."

I lived in an apartment next to an Albertsons supermarket. One day I was looking out the window and noticed they were throwing food away. I went to see what kind of food it was and saw all kinds of fruits and vegetables. I had hit the jackpot. So, I took home some boxes of fruits and vegetables and washed them.

For the next three months, people would come to teach the Word of God, and we would fellowship for hours. The fruit was ripe, and it was sweet and delicious. I didn't have the heart to tell them where it came from. 1 Thessalonians 5:18 (AMP) says, "in every situation [no matter what the circumstances] be thankful and continually give thanks to God; for this is the will of God for you in Christ Jesus."

I never let any of these terrible situations dictate my thoughts with doubt and fear. I stayed humble before the Lord. I just believed that God could do all things, and nothing was impossible for Him. I spent countless hours seeking the Lord because I couldn't get enough of Him.

As I was growing in my faith, I was seeing life the way a child would. A child trained in the things of God will develop pure faith and believe every word God says because the child has no worries, no cares, and no doubts. As adults we have responsibilities, and we see the worries and cares of this world.

God wants us to put all our trust in Him alone and to surrender all our worries and cares to Him. Psalm 55:22 (NASB) says, "Cast your burden upon the Lord and He will sustain you; He will never allow the righteous to be shaken."

And 1 Peter 5:7 (AMP) says, "casting all your cares [all your anxieties, all your worries, and all your concerns, once and for all] on Him, for He cares about you [with deepest affection, and watches over you very carefully]."

We have to trust the Lord the way Caleb did, so the Lord can say, "That person has a different spirit. He [she] has faith in me and follows me passionately and wholeheartedly."

To God be all the Glory!

Chapter 4
God Has a Sense of Humor With My Broken Car

1 Corinthians 1:27 (NIV) says, "But God chose the foolish things of the world to shame the wise; God chose the weak things of the world to shame the strong."

And Judges 7:2 (CEV) says, "The Lord said, 'Gideon, your army is too big. I can't let you win with this many soldiers. The Israelites would think that they had won the battle all by themselves and that I didn't have anything to do with it.'" Read the entire story in Judges 6 and 7.

Gideon had to trust God when things didn't seem to make sense in the natural world. This is the kind of faith God is looking for—men and women who are obedient and willing to act on His Word. Well, God had found his man, one who would trust and obey Him, no matter how ridiculous His instructions sounded.

The warriors God selected weren't mighty in strength or

skill. They were selected for knowing how to lap water like a dog. God has a sense of humor.

He didn't want the army of Israel to say, "Our mighty warriors defeated them with our strength and our wits." Reducing Gideon's army to 300 men to defeat an army of 130,000 meant they had to rely on God for victory.

Judges 7:12 (NIV) describes the enormity of the enemy's army this way: "The Midianites, the Amalekites and all the other eastern peoples had settled in the valley, thick as locusts. Their camels could no more be counted than the sand on the seashore." God is just showing us what He can do with a few men and women who obey Him.

Judges 7:16 (CEV) tells us how Gideon is going to fight this gigantic army. "Gideon divided his little army into three groups of 100 men, and he gave each soldier a trumpet and a large clay jar with a burning torch inside." We see God's humor in sending them into battle with horns, clay jars, and torches.

Judges 7:20 (CEV) tells us, "The rest of Gideon's soldiers blew the trumpets they were holding in their right hands. Then they smashed the jars and held the burning torches in their left hands. Everyone shouted, 'Fight with your swords for the Lord and for Gideon!'"

As you read the rest of the story, you see that God punishes His enemy by making them lose their minds and fight themselves.

God is Awesome!

I want you to see God's humor as you did in Gideon's

story. I believe that with God all things are possible. When I first got saved, I didn't have money to buy a good car. I ended up buying a broken car that overheated after driving two blocks. Every time I took a trip in that car, I would get in front of it and lay my hands on the hood and pray for a safe trip. Most people who saw me doing this would smirk at me, probably thinking I had lost my mind.

I started taking short trips to the store and saw that God was with me because the car never overheated even though my temperature gauge was in the red. So, I started praying for my car to go for an hour, then two hours, and it did without any problem.

So, I decided to take it on an eleven-hour journey from Oceanside, California, to El Paso, Texas, and I made it, so I knew God was with me. I would pray for my car to go back to California again, and I never experienced any problems.

One day a friend of mine shared with me that his mother was sick and he wanted to see her, but she lived in El Paso. So, I said to him, "I will take you. I have a car and it runs well." So, we decided to leave that weekend.

We were already out of San Diego when he noticed my temperature gauge was in the red. He said, "The car is overheating. Pull over before you ruin it."

I said, "No, I already prayed for my car, and we are going to have a safe trip to El Paso." I could sense the fear all over him, so I asked him, "Who made the sky?"

He responded, "God made the sky."

I asked him, "Who made the trees and grass?

He responded, "God did."

I asked, "Do you believe the God who made these incredible things can make this car go to El Paso?"

He said, "God can do all things but...."

I quickly cut him off and said, "No buts. He is." This is faith in action believing that God will give me a safe trip. When acting in faith, we have to stand on the Word for His promises. I didn't want doubts and fears coming in between God and me.

We made it to El Paso.

Four days later I picked him up so we could head back to California. He was very cheerful because he had just seen his family. We started driving back, and again he noticed my temperature gauge and told me my car was overheating. I smiled and asked him, "Who made the sun and the moon?"

He just put his hand up and said, "Ok." He didn't want me telling him what God can do.

I made three round trips from California to El Paso, and I drove all over California for six months before I took my car to a radiator shop. One of the mechanics told me, "Be glad you brought it in because your radiator is completely shot." *If he only knew how long I have been driving it with a bad radiator*, I thought.

With a smile I told him I was glad I had brought it in for him to put a new radiator in it. As I sat there, I pondered God's humor on how He made it possible for me to drive this car with a bad radiator for so long. There is nothing impossible with God. All things are possible if we believe.

Faith is having complete confidence and trust in God, knowing we can depend on Him to do what He says He will do. Hebrews 11:6 (KJV) says, "But without faith it is impossible to please Him, for he who comes to God must believe that He is, and that He is a rewarder of those who diligently seek Him."

The spiritual senses are invisible. Faith makes the invisible visible. That's the kind of faith that God requires, a faith that trusts in His Word. We are to think faith, speak faith, act faith, and keep the faith until the promise is fulfilled. I want to trust God just like Gideon, even when things in the natural world don't make sense.

To God be all the Glory!

Chapter 5
The Joy of the Spirit

Having God's inner peace is having an intimate relationship with Christ, and this brings us the glorious joy that the Holy Spirit gives. This spiritual joy brings a deep sense of delight within our inner man.

Galatians 5:22-23 (AMP) says, "But the fruit of the Spirit [the result of His presence within us] is love [unselfish concern for others], joy, [inner] peace, patience [not the ability to wait, but how we act while waiting], kindness, goodness, faithfulness, gentleness, self-control. Against such things there is no law."

And Romans 15:13 (GNT) says, "May God, the source of hope, fill you with all joy and peace by means of your faith in him, so that your hope will continue to grow by the power of the Holy Spirit."

As our relationship with Christ grows, we start reflecting His character, and the fruit of the Holy Spirit is evidence of His presence within us. Here we see the fruit of the Spirit is joy, and the joy of the Lord is our strength. Jesus makes this comment about joy in John 15:11 (AMP): "I have told you these things so that My joy *and* delight may be in you, and that your joy may be made full *and* complete *and* overflowing."

When I first heard the gospel, it was a small mission outreach in Los Angeles that would witness to me. They would invite me to their outings even though I was not saved. It was like a big picnic; they would play softball or volleyball and bring food and drinks. Even though I did not know Christ, I could see Christ's presence within them.

This mission outreach was God's handiwork in reaching out and witnessing to people like me. They were unselfish and always had a concern for others. Ephesians 2:10 (NIV) says, "For we are God's handiwork, created in Christ Jesus to do good works, which God prepared in advance for us to do."

Four years later I was saved in Oceanside, California. The church I attended had no sense of joy. It was just a bunch of older folks who believed in lots of manmade rules and "do's and don'ts." Now, they may have been saved, but they didn't believe God wanted us to enjoy life; everything was a sin. Many of these members had their joy gauge on empty or running on fumes, and they didn't even realize it.

I have seen so many defeated Christians, who have lost their joy. Many of them are so bogged down with worries and problems they don't realize the thief has come and stolen, killed, or destroyed their joy. We all have a spiritual gauge that measures our joy. All we have to do is look in the mirror. Only we can determine whether it is empty, full, or half full. Christ has given us life with joy and abundance.

In John 10:10 (The Voice), "The thief approaches with malicious intent, looking to steal, slaughter, and destroy; I came to give life with joy and abundance."

As our relationship with Christ grows, we start reflecting His character, and the fruit of the Holy Spirit is evidence of His presence within us. As long as we keep our eyes fixed on Christ by doing what He commands, we will never lose that glorious joy. When I look at myself in the mirror and my gauge is running low, I usually make a trip to spend a few days with my brother, Hector. We can talk about the Lord for fifteen hours straight, iron sharpening iron, and after a few days I feel my spiritual gauge filling up.

We need to put Christ first in our lives and seek Him will all our inner being to experience His joy. Devotional time with God allows us to recalibrate our hearts to His. That's why we need to make time to devote ourselves to the Lord and to rejoice in His presence.

Isaiah 60:1 (AMP) says:

> Arise [from spiritual depression to a new life], shine [be radiant with the glory and brilliance of the Lord]; for your light has come, And the glory and brilliance of the Lord has risen upon you. For in fact, darkness will cover the earth And deep darkness will cover the peoples; But the Lord will rise upon you [Jerusalem] And His glory and brilliance will be seen on you.

To God be all the Glory!

Chapter 6
Four Stages of Salvation

God's Word is life to us and to those we witness to. When we hear the message of God, we are to retain His Word in the center of our hearts, be obedient to His commandments, and be persistent until we bear fruit. This is the salvation and subsequent growth and maturity the parable of the farmer scattering seed talks about in Matthew 13, Mark 4, and Luke 8, which happens in four stages.

Stage One: Hearing the Word

Luke 8:12 (AMP) says, "Those beside the road are the people who have heard; then the devil comes and takes the message [of God] away from their hearts, so that they will not believe [in Me as the Messiah] and be saved."

When I first heard the Gospel of salvation, I enjoyed listening to it and I wanted it, but I heard another voice within me saying if I received it, I would lose the pleasures of life (sin) that I enjoyed. This was the evil one snatching away what others had sown in my heart. Nevertheless, I made a conscious effort to continue listening to the Word of God until I finally passed stage one and went on to the next stage.

Stage Two: Being Rooted in the Word

Matthew 13:20-21 (AMP) says:
> The one on whom seed was sown on rocky ground, this is the one who hears the word and at once welcomes it with joy; yet he has no [substantial] root in himself, but is only temporary, and when pressure or persecution comes because of the word, immediately he stumbles and falls away [abandoning the One who is the source of salvation].

When I welcomed salvation into my heart, I took hold of it, but I wasn't yet rooted to the Word of God, partly because everybody around me was making fun of me and harassing me because of the Word. 1 Peter 4:4 (GNT) says, "And now the heathen are surprised when you do not join them in the same wild and reckless living, and so they insult you."

I didn't want to lose the love, peace, and joy inside me. I had never felt anything like it. But the trials and persecution had begun. That was when I suffered my back injury and my pay got cut to nothing for three months straight. That was when I borrowed money from all my friends to stay alive, and I ended up eating out of Albertson's dumpster for three months.

But I never let my situation interfere with my relationship with the Lord. I wanted more and more of Him and felt as though I was wrapped in the Lord Himself. It was as though I had a forcefield around me, and I felt God's Spirit continuously over me. Without realizing it, God was rooting me in His Word. By staying focused on the Lord, I passed stage two and went forward to stage three.

Stage Three: The Lure of Wealth

Luke 8:14 (AMP) says, "The seed which fell among the thorns, these are the ones who have heard, but as they go on their way they are suffocated with the anxieties and riches and pleasures of this life, and they bring no fruit to maturity."

When I was a young believer, well-meaning Christian friends offered me a better job so I could drive a luxurious car and have a large home so that when people saw me, they would see that God had blessed me. But I told them all I wanted were the spiritual things of God rather than the glamour of this world.

The jobs they offered me, which could have afforded me a better home, required the time I needed to testify and witness to the lost souls in San Antonio. I needed a job I could leave when I wanted so I could attend to the things of God.

My car, which they referred to as the "jalopy," got me from point A to point B, and that's all I needed. Any time I visited the brothers in the Lord, they would tell me to park it in the back because they thought it was a disgrace and they didn't want anyone seeing it at their office.

By focusing on the Lord, I wasn't allowing the world to choke out the Word God had instilled in me. I finally passed stage three and went forward to stage four.

Stage Four: Bearing Fruit

Luke 8:15 (GNT) says, "The seeds that fell in good soil stand for those who hear the message and retain it in a good and obedient heart, and they persist until they bear fruit."

From the day I was saved I wanted everybody to have what I had: the love, joy, and peace that only God gives. I would tell people if they could only see what I see—that glorious joy, that wonderful peace—they would want it. I would tell them if I could pull out my eyes so they could see what I see, they would understand the love of God and what God wants for them. I stayed persistent by witnessing and testifying to anyone God put in front of me. I wanted everyone to have what I had, that special relationship with Christ Himself.

The more we want from this world, the less we will do for God. Accumulating the glamour and the riches of this world prevents us from witnessing and testifying for the Lord, making us unfruitful. Becoming successful in business means living at work and not having time for anything else. Matthew 6:21 says our time will be where our hearts are. Christ says in John 15:5 (NKJV), "I am the vine, you are the branches. He who abides in Me, and I in him, bears much fruit; for without Me you can do nothing."

If you're a Christian, you came back to life again when Christ did, and you're a new person. You are now "married," so to speak, to the one who rose from the dead so that you can produce good fruit, that is, good deeds for God.

We need to be persistent until we bear fruit for the kingdom of God. God's Word is life to us and to those we witness to.

To God be all the Glory!

Chapter 7
A Ruthless Family

If you have never read the story of Joseph, read Genesis 37, beginning in verse 26 (CEV): "Let's sell him to the Ishmaelites and not harm him. After all, he is our brother. And the others agreed." Verse 28 continues with, "When the Midianite merchants came by, Joseph's brothers took him out of the well, and for 20 pieces of silver they sold him to the Ishmaelites who took him to Egypt."

On my second enlistment in the military, I had to board a ship for six weeks. There is no privacy on a ship. We were stuffed in like sardines, four layers of bunk beds two feet apart on one side and another four layers of bunk beds on the other side. If we tried to get off the bunks at the same time, we rubbed against each other.

As I read the story of Joseph, I felt as though someone had just ripped my heart out. I cried. I know the other Marines in their bunks heard me crying, but none of them said anything.

I have seen so many dysfunctional families, but I have never seen a family as ruthless as Joseph's. My family came close. Being wild got me into lots of trouble. I was facing four months in jail, but my stepmother had connections with the judge. So she convinced him to make me join the military without my consent.

My other choice was to spend four months in jail (and not graduate from high school). So, I enlisted in the military for four years. They told me I was irresponsible and needed to grow up. "It is for your own good," was all I heard them say.

So, off to the military I went, and to my surprise, I discovered most of the other Marines were just like I was, irresponsible and wild. Being in the military is like being an indentured servant. I had to serve my time until I had completed my contract.

My mom and my dad had been divorced since I was six. My mother was a bitter and unhappy woman who wanted me to experience the same bitterness she had. It was like a poison. She enjoyed killing someone's spirit so that person could feel her misery.

The words of a bitter person are frightening and do considerable damage to a child. They sound something like this: "You're going to be just like your father, a good-for-nothing drunk. I don't know why I carried you to full term. You should have never been born. You will never amount to anything. You're too dumb and stupid. Don't give me that look, or I will slap it off." That's what I had to live with.

Ephesians 4:29 (NIV) says, "Do not let any unwholesome

talk come out of your mouths, but only what is helpful for building others up according to their needs, that it may benefit those who listen."

Despite the negativity, I still enjoyed life. Even when I was in and out of jail, I was always having fun. My family would always say, "You only live once, so enjoy."

My dad was a good man, but his favorite saying throughout my childhood was, "Son, there are three things in life you need to know: beer, women, and money." He told me these three things would bring me happiness.

Well, I grabbed it and ran with it. I discovered that life was hard, but I still followed my dad's advice because I still believed it even though it was far from the truth. I would go to a club to dance, drink beer, and allegedly "have a good time." As I said earlier, many times, to my surprise, I would walk out of a club, and someone would be shooting at me.

Many of the women were married and somehow "forgot" to disclose that information. Sometimes I would be dancing and having a good ol' time, and I would smile at some pretty lady walking by. Next thing I knew I was in a fight because someone didn't like that I smiled at his wife or girlfriend.

Many times, I would be driving my car and the police would stop me because I was drinking and driving. I thought they were just harassing me for no reason.

Obviously, following my dad's advice didn't bring me happiness. I didn't know what it was to be happy until God saved me and gave me inner peace in my spirit. That's when I found true happiness.

My dad never showed me love or affection. He was always harsh with his words. I know he loved me but he didn't know how to show it. I could talk to him for hours, especially about sports.

On his death bed, my aunt and I talked about how we never grew up with love. She said, "You should let your dad know that you love him."

So, when he awoke from his sleep I told him, "You know that I love you."

He got frustrated and said, "Oh no, what are you saying?" and turned his back to me because he didn't understand how one man could tell another man that he loved him.

While he was in hospice care, one of the nurses from the nursing home would call me and say, "It looks like your dad is passing away."

I would rush to see him, and to my surprise, he would wake up and ask me, "What is going on?" This went on for a month, and I finally asked him if he was afraid of dying. He said he was, so I taught him the Word of God. I praise God that my dad accepted Christ as his personal Savior on his death bed. The fear of dying was gone, and he had the peace of God in him.

From that point on, each day, before he passed, he would tell me he was in heaven, looking at a giant door, but nobody was there. He said the door didn't have a handle or a knob, so he couldn't open it.

But on the day he passed, he said, "I was in front of that giant door, and there was a knob. I pushed it, and the door opened, and I started going in. But I came back to let you know that I am going in, and I might not be coming back." We said our goodbyes to each other, and He fell asleep and died.

We don't realize the authority we have as parents. Our children believe what we tell them because it is coming from someone with authority. Being mistreated produced hate in me, and my anger showed. Colossians 3:21 (AMP) says:

> Fathers, do not provoke or irritate or exasperate your children [with demands that are trivial or unreasonable or humiliating or abusive; nor by favoritism or indifference; treat them tenderly with lovingkindness], so they will not lose heart and become discouraged or unmotivated [with their spirits broken].

After my mind had been twisted and confused for such a long time, the Lord took all the anger and hate out of me. Titus 3:4-5 (NLT) says, "When God our Savior revealed his kindness and love, he saved us, not because of the righteous things we had done, but because of his mercy. He washed away our sins, giving us a new birth and new life through the Holy Spirit."

Those of us born in messed-up families don't necessarily turn out badly. Joseph overcame his situation and trusted the Lord. James 4:8 (AMP) tells us to "Come close to God with a contrite heart and He will come close to you...."

I praise and glorify my Lord for being the Savior of my life!

By Alex Valenzuela

Chapter 8
God Healed My Back Injury

Hebrews 11:1 (AMP) says, "Now faith is the assurance (title deed, confirmation) of things hoped for (divinely guaranteed), and the evidence of things not seen [the conviction of their reality—faith comprehends as fact what cannot be experienced by the physical senses]."

I lived in constant pain for a year after my back injury in 1986. Three discs on my back were ready to rupture and I was taking opioids and valium.

The more I learned about Christ, the more I had a burning desire to witness, and I saw many people come to the Lord. With that same burning desire I started to pray for the sick and I saw the Lord heal them. But for some reason He never healed me.

In 1987, the Lord told me to move to San Antonio, Texas, and I obeyed. I met some Christian brothers who believed in healing and prayed for me. But nothing happened because it was a gradual healing, not a miracle healing, and I had to believe. But I believed that God was the healer, and I was healed.

I had a burning sensation within me to search the scriptures about healing and the power of God. I pondered John 10:10, which says, the devil comes to steal, kill, and destroy, and I realized he was trying to destroy my spirit. But I was so active in witnessing that I didn't care about pain, so I didn't feel sorry for myself.

The longer the sickness stayed in my body, the more the devil tried to steal, kill, and destroy my spirit. Consequently, he started stealing the joy from me, along with all the promises the Lord had given me, and he tried to make me doubt that Christ is the healer. But then I pondered what Jesus said in John 10:10 that "I am come that they might have life, and that they might have it more abundantly." Living in misery is not a life of abundance.

I made up my mind to declare war on the devil for my healing. I scattered pages of scriptures throughout the house. Every time my back pain flared up, I fell to the ground for an hour or two to relieve the pain, took the pages in my hand, and started quoting the scriptures.

I found myself telling the devil that he is a liar, but I had to make sure I didn't make the little lying devil greater than God. God created all things that exist, even that little lying devil. Colossians 2:13-15 (NLT) says:

> You were dead because of your sins and because your sinful nature was not yet cut away. Then God made you alive with Christ, for he forgave all our sins. He canceled the record of the charges against us and took

it away by nailing it to the cross. In this way, he disarmed the spiritual rulers and authorities. He shamed them publicly by his victory over them on the cross.

Christ lives in me, and I am alive. I kept reminding the devil that God made him, God made me, and God says I am healed. Yes, I am healed!

I would say, "Do you understand, you little lying devil, that I am healed by His stripes because He has stripped you of all your powers? 2 Corinthians 2:11 (AMP) tells me 'to keep Satan from taking advantage of us; for we are not ignorant of his schemes.' It is written. God has stripped you of all your powers. You are powerless, you little lying devil. Ephesians 6:16 (GNT) says, 'At all times carry faith as a shield; for with it you will be able to put out all the burning arrows shot by the Evil One.' Depart from me, you little lying devil. You have nothing on me."

The more I did this, the worse the pain got. But I couldn't be occupied with the symptoms or the feelings, because that would have turned off the switch to God's power. This was a war, and I was in my trench, fighting for my healing for thirty straight days. I meditated on God's Word, and I pondered it until it bloomed in my heart.

The inner man, which is the soul, picked up on it and believed. My soul and spirit were one, connected with God's Spirit, and healing just came into my body. On the thirty-first day, the pain was gone. I wish God had given me a miracle healing, but I had to trust in Him and His promises with His Word.

Hebrews 13:15 says, "Therefore by Him let us continually offer the sacrifice of praise to God, that is, the fruit of our lips, giving thanks to His name."

And Jonah 2:8 (KJV) says "They that observe lying vanities forsake their own mercy. But I will sacrifice unto thee with the voice of thanksgiving; I will pay that that I have vowed. Salvation is of the Lord."

No matter how hard I fought for my healing, my situation could never compare to Jonah being inside a whale. Jonah teaches us not to look at the situation we are in, but to observe lying vanities that cause us to forsake our own mercy.

Then he offers the voice of thanksgiving. If we want God to respond to our sickness, we need to act on our faith for God to manifest our healing. We need to know who we are in the kingdom of God, dig our trench, and fight for what is ours. We need to say not only that "I am born of God," but that "I am a partaker of God's nature and life. I have Christ dwelling in me and the Spirit of Him who raised Christ from the dead dwelling in me. By His stripes I am healed."

As soon as the Spirit in us sees it and embraces it, our spirits will respond.

I praise and glorify God for His tender mercy!

Chapter 9
Giving by Faith

Hebrews 11:1-3 (NKJV) says, "Now faith is the substance of things hoped for, the evidence of things not seen. For by it the elders obtained a good testimony. By faith we understand that the worlds were framed by the word of God, so that the things which are seen were not made of things which are visible."

When God told me to move from California to San Antonio, Texas, in 1987, I had no idea why He wanted me there. I had no family, friends, or job. Like Abraham I was making a trip to the unknown. Genesis 12:1,4 (KJV) says:

> Now the Lord had said unto Abram, Get thee out of thy country, and from thy kindred, and from thy father's house, unto a land that I will shew thee: So Abram departed, as the Lord had spoken unto him; and Lot went with him: and Abram was seventy and five years old when he departed out of Haran.

Can you imagine the love and reverence Abraham had for God? He was willing to follow God's command at age seventy-five. Lord, I pray you will give me Abraham's strength to follow you the way he did.

I got lost quite a bit trying to find my way around San Antonio. One day I stopped and asked three men at a church if they would help me get to where I was going. As they gave directions, we started talking about the Lord, and they invited me to church that evening. So, I went home, changed, and hurried back to the service.

As I sat in the back and listened to the message, the Lord spoke to my spirit, and said, "Give a thousand dollars." The Lord knew I had only eighty dollars to my name, but He kept telling me to give a thousand dollars. I was stepping into the unknown of giving.

When God tells us to give, we shouldn't fight it. Hebrews 13:16 (AMP) tells us, "Do not neglect to do good, to contribute to the needy of the church as an expression of fellowship, for such sacrifices are always pleasing to God." We shouldn't ask whether it is of God, because the lying little devil will never tell us to give money for the things of God.

After the service was over, I introduced myself to the pastor and told him what God had said to me, "On Sunday morning you shall have the money I am giving you to give to the church." I told him that God was using my lips as an instrument to speak those words, so I knew He was going to make it happen. I told the pastor, "I don't have the money, and I don't know where it is coming from, but I know one thing: God spoke it and I believe it, so I will be here Sunday morning to give you the money."

Faith never waits to see before it believes. It is the evidence of things not seen. Faith is having complete trust in God, knowing we can depend on Him to do what He says He will do. "Thus saith the Lord" settles everything. "It is written" is all that faith needs. When we stand firm on God's Word and He tells us to do something, we need to just do it by stepping into action by saying it.

By Saturday morning I was praising and thanking God for the money. Psalm 37:4-5 (NKJV) says, "Delight yourself also in the Lord, And He shall give you the desires of your heart. Commit your way to the Lord, Trust also in Him, And He shall bring it to pass."

As I was praising and thanking God, I heard the mailman putting mail in my box. When I pulled the mail out of the box, I noticed a check for a large amount of money, so I took it to the bank and deposited it. On Sunday morning I put a check into the offering plate.

The pastor dismissed the service, and I saw the usher rushing toward him to give him a piece of paper. The pastor called the church members back and told them to sit. He said, "I have a confession" and explained what had occurred at the Wednesday night service.

He said, "A stranger came to me on Wednesday night and said he was going to give the church a thousand dollars on Sunday morning. He said he was broke but believed that God was going to provide the money. He told me that God was using his lips as an instrument to speak the words.

I thought he was off his rocker. I said to myself, 'How many times have I heard this?' They mean well but have no money. Brothers and sisters, I repent for doubting because here is the check for a thousand dollars. Ephesians 3:20 (NLT) says, 'Now all glory to God, who is able, through his mighty power at work within us, to accomplish infinitely more than we might ask or think.'"

The church service got so quiet it was as if the members were attending a funeral. Suddenly one man stood up and said, "Pastor, here is a thousand dollars."

Another man stood up and said, "Pastor, here is a thousand dollars." This went on until they finally decided to collect an offering.

After they counted the offering, the pastor said they collected more than $110,000. They had been praying for money to build an addition for the church because it was too small.

When God is in the midst, He will do what He says He will do. I learned that when God tells me to do something to just do it without thinking about it so that doubt does not creep in. God is our provider. He is Jehovah-Jireh!

I praise and glorify the Lord for watching over me!

Chapter 10
Joy in the Midst

John 15:11-12 (GNT) says, "I have told you this so that my joy may be in you and that your joy may be complete. My commandment is this: love one another, just as I love you."

Many people think joy and happiness are the same, but they are not. Joy is the fruit of the Holy Spirit within us. This is a deep sense of delight within our inner man. Happiness is an external emotion based on circumstances.

One of the greatest blessings I have ever received was two brothers in the Lord, Ralph and Frank, who had the same burning desire I had to witness and testify. Jeremiah 20:9 (GNT) says, "…then your message is like a fire burning deep within me…." We stayed as one, and when hard times came our way, we were always there to strengthen each other.

We regularly witnessed on the streets of San Antonio, but it still felt as though we weren't doing enough for the kingdom of God. One day my brother, Ralph, asked me if I wanted to go to the prison to witness. At first, I was reluctant to go, so I said I would pray about it.

Then one night the Lord gave me a dream about a cousin who was like a brother to me. In the dream I saw him, and I tried to give him a hug, but he pushed me away and turned his back. I asked him, "What is wrong?"

He said, "Where were you when I needed you most? I was in prison, and you never visited me, you never prayed for me, and you never gave me money to buy a snack. Well, cuz, what do you have to say for yourself?"

I woke up feeling so guilty because he was right. I hadn't done any of this. So the same day I filled out and mailed the application to minister in the prison.

At the same time, I went to minister to my cousin in prison at Santa Fe, New Mexico. When he saw me, he saw how God had changed my life. We talked about God and what he was doing in my life. He had so many questions, but our time was limited there. He asked me to pray for him, and I lifted my arms toward heaven and prayed.

The power of God hit my cousin like a lightning bolt and knocked him to the ground. He got up with fear in his eyes and said, "Why did you hit me?"

I replied to him, "I did not touch you. It was the power of God that knocked you down."

He said, "I had never felt anything as powerful as that."

I told him that God loved him and wanted to be part of his life. I never understood why God demonstrated His power like that to him. Now by visiting him I had a sense of relief, and I didn't feel guilty like I did in my dream.

The prison ministry allowed us to teach the Word of God inside the prison for three days. I felt as though we had just won the lottery. When the day finally arrived that we were going to be witnessing in one of the prisons around Houston, I was so excited.

But when I went to Ralph and Frank's house, their car wouldn't start. The little lying devil was trying to prevent us from witnessing. Paul mentions an opportunity for witnessing and the opposition that comes with it in 1 Corinthians 16:9 (NLT): "There is a wide-open door for a great work here, although many oppose me."

We had two choices. We could stay home and do nothing or go without a car. We decided to hitchhike. We rode in the back of a pickup from San Antonio all the way to Houston. Life was throwing us a curve ball, and we learned to make the best of it. We just huddled up together and talked about the things of God (iron sharpening iron). These were the most joyful times of our lives when we felt the presence of the Lord in the midst of us.

When we got to the location, the three of us barely scraped up enough money to get one hotel room. Flipping the coin was the only way to see who would win the grand prize of sleeping on the bed. As we were there, we would gather with other brothers from different parts of the state. Usually thirty people would go into the prison, and we would share Christ until two or three in the morning.

After witnessing all day in the prison the next day, we went to our room, and we were hungry. We started emptying our pockets to see how much money we had and found we had enough money to buy a bucket of chicken that would last us two days.

We witnessed in the prisons for about a year and a half and saw many men give their lives to Christ. Neither I nor the two brothers with me had full-time jobs, but God always supplied our needs. I cannot count how many times the enemy tried to stop us from witnessing or testifying. We were always fighting that little lying devil.

On one of our trips to the prison we found ourselves riding in the back of a pickup again, and it started pouring rain. Imagine being soaking wet and shivering from the cold air. This was the worst trip that I can remember. We were blessed to have eaten on this trip because we often had to fast until we got home.

God can cause our inner man to be full of joy even when things on the outside aren't pleasant. Paul speaks of the hard times he went through in 2 Corinthians 11:27 (NLT): "I have worked hard and long, enduring many sleepless nights. I have been hungry and thirsty and have often gone without food. I have shivered in the cold, without enough clothing to keep me warm."

We counted it as joy to participate in the Lord's work. Christ makes it clear that we will share in the reward that comes from every seed we sow. Ephesians 2:10 (NIV) says, "For we are God's handiwork, created in Christ Jesus to do good works, which God prepared in advance for us to do."

So many Christians have said to me, "We are so blessed, and we have never had problems like that." I guarantee the more we testify and the more we witness, the more we will see the attack of the little lying devil. We witnessed and testified daily.

I always remember what Christ said in John 15:5 (GNT): "I am the vine, and you are the branches. Those who remain in me, and I in them, will bear much fruit; for you can do nothing without me." We are supposed to be bearing fruit for the kingdom of God. If we aren't bearing fruit, we need to fix our spiritual lives.

We are united with the Lord in one spirit, we are the body of Christ, we are fully equipped, and we have the mind of Christ, so He can guide us with His thoughts.

Here are four scriptures that bear this out:

- 1 Corinthians 6:17 (AMP): "But the one who is united and joined to the Lord is one spirit with Him."
- 1 Corinthians 12:27 (NIV): "Now you are the body of Christ, and each one of you is a part of it."
- Ephesians 4:12 (AMP): "[and He did this] to fully equip and perfect the saints (God's people) for works of service, to build up the body of Christ [the church];"
- 1 Corinthians 2:16 (AMP): "...But we have the mind of Christ [to be guided by His thoughts and purposes]."

Since we are fully equipped with the power of Christ because He lives in us, why are most Christians sitting in the pews, doing nothing? We are to be witnessing, testifying, teaching, preaching, praying for the sick, and praying for the lost.

Christ can do nothing except through His body, and we are the body of Christ. Christ's Body is me! It is you! It is not a congregation or a denomination. The church is the body of Christ. He needs us to witness and win souls. So, go!

To God be all the Glory!

Chapter 11
No Spinal Cord

In 1989, two years after God had healed my back, one night I awoke and moved to stand up, but I couldn't feel my spinal cord. It felt as though the middle of my body was missing. I would step forward not knowing or understanding how I was doing it. It was as if there was no communication between the nerves in my spine cord and my brain.

Fear was trying to come into my mind and enslave me. Two scriptures came to mind:

- 2 Timothy 1:7 (NKJV), "For God has not given us a spirit of fear, but of power and of love and of a sound mind"
- Proverbs 3:5 (NIV), "Trust in the Lord with all your heart and lean not on your own understanding."

The little lying devil was at it again, trying to create fear within me. This was the time to rely on God and stand on His promises. 2 Corinthians 2:11 (The Voice) says, "It's my duty to make sure that Satan does not win even a small victory over us, for we don't want to be naïve and then fall prey to his schemes."

I didn't have time to do anything other than remember God's Word and His promises to me. Isaiah 41:10 (NIV) instructs us, "So do not fear, for I am with you; do not be dismayed, for I am your God. I will strengthen you and help you; I will uphold you with my righteous right hand."

I grabbed hold of God's righteous hand and didn't let go. I couldn't let fear dictate what the outcome would be, so I grabbed hold of God's Word, believing He would take care of me. Isaiah 41:13 (NIV) says, "For I am the Lord your God who takes hold of your right hand and says to you, Do not fear; I will help you."

I had to create a mindset for combatting this situation. First I shut myself off from everybody. I didn't know how long God would take to heal me, so I couldn't let anyone know what I was going through. I didn't want anything negative to come into my spirit, "to keep Satan from taking advantage of us; for we are not ignorant of his schemes" (2 Corinthians 2:11, AMP).

I knew this was going to be a fight between thought and intent, so my soul and spirit had to be united as one. This wasn't easy, but it was mind over matter. Psalm 112:6-8 (GNT) says, "…He is not afraid of receiving bad news; his faith is strong, and he trusts in the Lord. He is not worried or afraid; he is certain to see his enemies defeated."

The only thing in my favor was that I was constantly feeding my soul the Word of God. My stereo played nothing but praise and worship music and the Word of God day and night. I hardly ever watched TV. Each night, before I fell asleep, I played instrumental music as I meditated on the Word of God.

Ephesians 6:10-13 (GNT) says:

> Finally, build up your strength in union with the Lord and by means of his mighty power. Put on all the armor that God gives you, so that you will be able to stand up against the Devil's evil tricks. For we are not fighting against human beings but against the wicked spiritual forces in the heavenly world, the rulers, authorities, and cosmic powers of this dark age. So put on God's armor now!

And Ephesians 6:16 (GNT) continues with:

> At all times carry faith as a shield; for with it you will be able to put out all the burning arrows shot by the Evil One. And accept salvation as a helmet, and the word of God as the sword which the Spirit gives you.

When the Lord fights side by side with us, the devil's wiles cannot harm us. The little lying devil tries to make us think his tricks are real, that we were never healed in the first place. But God healed me completely of my back injury.

Two years later the little lying devil was trying to make me feel as if I had no spinal cord. In any circumstance, I can believe what I feel or believe what I know, which is the promises of God. We have the victory over Satan's schemes. We just have to know who we are in Christ.

This fight lasted three straight days and then it was gone. God is in control. We just need to trust Him. Hebrews 10:23 (AMP) tells us, "Let us seize and hold tightly the confession of our hope without wavering, for He who promised is reliable and trustworthy and faithful [to His word]."

Christ is trustworthy and faithful to His promises. We just need to grab hold of our confession and not waver. Faith is an action, and we have to believe His Word for it to manifest.

I praise and glorify the Lord and Savior of my soul!

Chapter 12
The Spirit Giveth Life And The Flesh Has To Obey

John 6:63 (AMP) says, "It is the Spirit who gives life; the flesh conveys no benefit [it is of no account]. The words I have spoken to you are spirit and life [providing eternal life]."

In 1989, I was working at one of the hotels forty-five minutes away from Orlando, Florida, constructing the entire fourteenth floor. The company I worked for would turn off the electrical power from the floor and provide their own electrical system, adding ground fault circuit interrupters, which is an electrical system built into a power cord to protect people from severe electrical shocks.

One sprinkler burst in one of the work areas, and I had to make sure all the workers evacuated the area. As the last worker was getting out, I felt an electrical shock. So, I jumped to relieve myself from the shock. I kept jumping toward the door to get out, but every time I hit the ground, I was shocked. Each shock felt as though it was going straight to my heart.

Little did we know that someone had turned on the electricity to the floor we were working on. The paramedics came and examined us to make sure we were ok. When one of them checked me, he Said. "This cannot be right." He thought something was wrong with his machine, so he rechecked me. He ended up taking me to the ambulance to examine me because he thought his machine was broken.

When we got to the ambulance, he told me to lie down, and he strapped me to the machine. He called the doctor on the phone, explained the readings, and then injected me with something to help me relax. He asked, Do you know the Lord Jesus Christ as your personal Savior?"

At that moment, the Lord spoke to me and said, "the Spirit giveth life and the flesh has to obey." So, I had to speak life from that moment. I couldn't let anything contrary to the Word of God come in me. Scriptures started coming to my mind such as:

- 1 Corinthians 6:17 (AMP) "But the one who is united and joined to the Lord is one spirit with Him."
- Luke 17:21 (GNT) "…because the Kingdom of God is within you,"
- John 14:16-17 (AMP) "He (the Holy Spirit) remains with you continually and will be in you."

God was in our midst, and I had to trust Him with all my inner being. I had to grab hold of Him and not let go. Regardless of what was showing on the monitor, I had to keep focused on what God was saying to me through His Word.

I said to the young man, "Yes, I know Him as my personal Savior. He just spoke to me and said the Spirit giveth life and the flesh has to obey."

He kept shaking his head as he was looking at the monitor. My condition must have looked pretty bleak. As he was mumbling to himself, I told him, "I assure you that nothing is going to happen to me."

He was having a hard time accepting the words God had given me because he was trained to believe medical science. The monitor was telling him I was going to die, and God was telling me I was going to live.

It took forty-five minutes to get to the hospital. Once we arrived, the staff wheeled me into the emergency room. There must have been ten to twelve doctors waiting for me, all asking me "Where does it hurt? What do you feel?"

I replied, "There is nothing wrong with me. My God said the Spirit giveth life and the flesh has to obey." I wasn't letting go of what the Lord had said to me.

I heard one of them say, "The damage from the electrical shock has damaged his mind." So they wheeled me into intensive care and strapped monitors to my chest.

That afternoon I asked the nurse when my meal was coming in. She said, "You are on a special diet and brought me onion soup."

I smiled and said, "Ok, what am I going to do now?" shaking my head because I was hungry. I decided to call Domino's Pizza, who delivered a pizza to my room. I must have ordered it during a shift change because no one paid attention. By the time the nurse walked in, I had already eaten half the pizza, and she rushed out of my room.

Then the doctor came in with the nurse and said to me, "Do you know how bad that is for you?"

I smiled and said, "I was hungry, and I prayed for it." He lectured me about my heart condition, and I just let him do it. I let him know that God had spoken to me and said the Spirit giveth life and the flesh has to obey, so there was nothing wrong with me. After that, he walked out the door without saying a word to me.

When I was in the hospital, one of the staff members would check my vital signs every hour. Every time I fell asleep, my heart rate would go down to thirty beats per minute. So, someone on staff would wake me and strap the EKG monitor to me. This must have happened five times the first night.

The second day I was in the hospital, they gave me several different tests, all of which I passed with flying colors. At lunch, they still had me on the onion soup diet, which I call the water diet. So, I called my boss and asked him to bring me a double cheeseburger with all the works. He came in with my order and we visited.

I was eating my cheeseburger when the nurse walked in and then back out the door. Once again, the doctor came in with the nurse and started lecturing me once again on how bad the cheeseburger was for me. And again, I told him, "I was hungry, and I prayed for it."

The doctor noticed how headstrong I was, so he decided to open the cafeteria to me. He told the nurse, "Give him what he wants. I don't want him eating from the restaurants."

I was bored out of my mind, just being in the room. So, with two different monitors strapped to my chest, I decided to do something productive. I pushed my IV pole down the hallway and knocked on doors to visit people in intensive care. I shared the Word of God with them, and they would ask me why I was in the hospital. I told them I'd had an accident at work and that I had been electrocuted. Then I would tell them, "They just have me here for observation because they just can't figure me out. Every time they look at the reading of the monitor, they look at me as if to say, 'What's keeping you alive?'"

I would witness to them by saying, "But my God spoke to me and said the Spirit giveth life and the flesh has to obey. I don't feel sick, and I know I am completely healed by His stripes." Then I started quoting Colossians 3:1-2 (NLT): "Since you have been raised to new life with Christ, set your sights on the realities of heaven, where Christ sits in the place of honor at God's right hand. Think about the things of heaven, not the things of earth."

Then I quoted James 1:6 (NLT) "...be sure that your faith is in God alone. Do not waver, for a person with divided loyalty is as unsettled as a wave of the sea that is blown and tossed by the wind." I believe what God says over any medical doctor or any monitor. That night was no different than the first night. They wouldn't let me sleep.

After I had completed my four-day stay in the hospital,

the doctor finally sat next to me, holding the test results in his hands and shaking his head. He said, "We just don't understand what is going on with your heart."

I smiled and said to him, "My doctor came in and said I was completely healed and there was nothing wrong with me."

He stood up and said, "Who was this doctor that told you this?"

And I replied, "His name is Dr. Jesus Christ."

He angrily walked out of the room, and the nurse came in with my discharge papers later that day.

1 Corinthians 2:16 (AMP) says, "…But we have the mind of Christ [to be guided by

His thoughts and purposes]," and Hebrews 10:23 (ASV) says, "Let us hold fast the confession of our hope that it waver not; for he is faithful that promised." Confession is simply believing with our hearts and repeating with our lips God's own declaration of who we are in Christ.

God had His hand on me while I was in the hospital, and everything the doctors had learned from medical science wasn't lining up with what they were seeing. God has the outcome in our lives, but we have to trust Him at His Word, and His words to me were "The spirit giveth life and the flesh has to obey."

To God be all the Glory!

Chapter 13
The Call To Evangelize

2 Chronicles 16:9 (CEV) says, "The Lord is constantly watching everyone, and he gives strength to those who faithfully obey him...."

In 1990 God was calling me to go and evangelize in Mexico, and this is how He confirmed it to me.

I visited a nearby Spanish church to hear the Word. At the end of the service the pastor called me to the front, and said, "God has a word for you." He started prophesying over me by saying "God wants you to go into Mexico and preach the good news." He started crying and said, "I see hard times that you must endure there, and you will see what most people only dream of seeing because the power of the Holy Spirit will be with you." I took the prophecy to heart and pondered it. Now I wanted confirmation from God on this.

Several weeks later I was invited to a revival, and there was so much excitement in the praise and worship service. The guest speaker at the revival was a black evangelist. I listened to the sermon, and at the end he called me to the front and had almost the same exact message as the Spanish church. Now I knew that God was calling me because there was confirmation. I started praying on how to go about it. I didn't know anyone in Mexico or how to start. Several scriptures came to mind as I pondered his message:

- 1 Peter 2:21 (AMP) "For [as a believer] you have been called for this purpose, since Christ suffered for you, leaving you an example, so that you may follow in His footsteps."
- John 10:27 (AMP) "The sheep that are My own hear My voice *and* listen to Me; I know them, and they follow Me."

Again a few weeks went by, and I was at my church, and we had a special speaker from Houston, and he was a prophet. At the end of the service he called me to the front and said, "God has a word for you." He said, "God is calling you to go and preach the good news in Mexico. God is saying to let go of everything that you value so much and go, for He will take care of you." Now this was the third man giving me the same message, and all three men that gave me the message had never met me and did not know each other.

What was hard for me was that I was part owner of a demolition company, and we were striving. I worked so hard to build it up and now the Lord wanted me to let it go. I knew it was God telling me to go, but this meant I had to let go of my company and trust God by faith. This decision is practically impossible for most people because they will choose the luxury of the world.

That same night a man approached me and said, "My name is Brother Joe, and God called me to come here and let you know that you will not be going alone into Mexico. I am going with you, and I will be your mentor." God was putting all the pieces together, and on January 1, 1991, we left for Mexico.

Brother Joe was an older man, and he was an evangelist with the gift of prophecy, kind of like Silas in Acts 15:32. In my ministry God had given me a greater measure of the gift of faith, and I was willing to act on it.

1 Corinthians 12:4-6 (NLT) says, "There are different kinds of spiritual gifts, but the same Spirit is the source of them all. There are different kinds of service, but we serve the same Lord. God works in different ways, but it is the same God who does the work in all of us. A spiritual gift is given to each of us so we can help each other."

We were so different in how we saw things, but together we were a powerful ministry in maximizing our spiritual gifts for preaching the gospel. The two of us were able to establish and teach the Word of God effectively to both men and women.

I had never seen a man pray as hard as brother Joe; he would pray a good eight hours a day. He would search for the Lord with all his inner being. He would cry for the lost souls like someone losing their mother.

As we traveled through Mexico, I found myself seeking the Lord most of the night and slept very little. We had two or three teachings throughout the day and one-night services, and this went on for all of 1991. I saw God perform countless miracles every day for that whole year.

There were more brothers in the Lord that joined us throughout that year. We were just letting God have His way in what He wanted to do. In the next several pages, I will give some accounts of what I saw.

I praise and glorify God, and give Him all the glory.

Chapter 14
Christ Liveth in Me

2 Corinthians 3:18 (TLB)"...we can be mirrors that brightly reflect the glory of the Lord. And as the Spirit of the Lord works within us, we become more and more like him."

Receiving Christ into my life brought many adventures with the Lord. Every time I came home, I visited my grandma, and she would say, "Tell me about one of your adventures with God." So, I would visit with her for hours, telling her what God was doing in my life. She just couldn't get enough and wanted more.

One day I was visiting her, and she said, "Tell me about your adventures with God."

I told her, "My brother is in town. Let him tell you about his adventures with God."

She said, "Your God is alive in you, and he comes out of you. Your brother is saved, and we have seen his changes, but there is a difference between the two of you." It reminded me of Numbers 14:24 (The Voice): "For Caleb, though, it's a different matter. He's distinct from the others by having a different spirit and has followed My lead wholeheartedly...."

Her comment bothered me for a while because I didn't understand. The Lord transformed my brother into a new man, and I saw that with my own eyes. The only difference was that we both took different paths in the Lord.

Years later I realized what my grandma was saying: to be close to God, we have to spend time with Him.

Galatians 2:20 (ASV) says, "I have been crucified with Christ; and it is no longer I that live, but Christ liveth in me"

And Luke 17:21 (KJV) says, "...the Kingdom of God is within you."

My grandmother used to tell me, "If I ever get sick, I want you to pray for me because I know the God who lives in you will heal me."

In 1988 I received a call from a family member saying they had put our grandmother in the hospital, her kidneys had failed her, and she would be on kidney dialysis for the rest of her life.

The following day I drove nine hours to go see her. I walked into the room she was in, and said, "Grandma, the God that you see coming out of me is going to heal you right now." I put my hands on her and commanded healing to come upon her kidneys.

The power of God was so strong that she started saying, "I'm healed; I'm healed. I feel a warmth all over my body." They did a test on her kidneys and said she was completely healed. She never had dialysis after that. Praise be to God.

In 1991 my grandmother ended up in the hospital again. She was in a coma, but I didn't know. I was three weeks into a thirty-day fast. A brother in the Lord had loaned us a house, so I wouldn't be disturbed while I was fasting. Brother Joe and brother Hector came to where I was and said, "Your grandmother is in the hospital. She has been in a coma for twenty-one days, and if you want to see her before she dies, you need to go."

I turned in my fast to the Lord and drove about six hours to the hospital. When I arrived, I went to her room, and it felt like a morgue. I sat and listened to the family, all non-believers, speaking death into her. They wouldn't speak to me because they were afraid I was going to preach salvation to them.

After everyone left, I walked up to her and commanded her spirit to return to her. She started gasping for air and then she started crying. She said, "While I was in the coma, I could hear all the conversations. I know which dress I will be wearing when I die."

I loved to joke with my grandmother, so I said to her, "I came from far away and you don't have anything for me to eat."

She pointed toward the nurse's station and said, "You tell them to release me, and I will fix you something to eat."

My grandmother was seventy-six and had abdominal cancer. I asked her if she wanted God to heal her and she replied, "Yes." I prayed against the cancer and God healed her.

The lady on the other side of the curtain said, "Can you pray for me?" She said she had a heart problem, and I asked her if she believed Christ would heal her. She replied, "Yes, I believe." As I prayed for her, I felt the power of God heal her.

The next day I went to see my grandmother. The nurse said she threw up through the night and said it was green. I explained to her it was the cancer coming out. I asked about the other lady, and the nurse said she was completely healed. She was discharged that morning.

To God be all the Glory!

When I saw my grandmother, she just looked so happy. She had life in her again. She was eating and visiting with everyone there. She was completely healed.

My grandmother knew if I prayed for her, she would be healed. It is our faith in Christ that makes us well, and she saw the Spirit of the Lord living in me. Galatians 2:20 (AMP) says, "it is no longer I who live, but Christ lives in me." She wasn't looking at me to heal her. She was looking at the One living in me to heal her. She had developed faith in action like the woman in Mark 5:28 (NKJV), who said, "If only I may touch His clothes, I shall be made well."

After the woman in the Bible was healed, she started telling other people, "Just touch His garment, and you will be healed." People started listening to her testimony and doing just that. Matthew 14:36 (NIV) says, "They begged him to let the sick touch at least the fringe of his robe, and all who touched him were healed."

When we put our faith in action and believe in Him, we see His power to heal. Hebrews 13:8 (NKJV) says, "Jesus

Christ is the same yesterday, today, and forever."

I praise and glorify my Lord!

One day we were preaching in a revival, and during the service one lady started praising God. With excitement she was saying, "It is gone! It is gone!" as she was rubbing her husband's stomach.

She started crying and the whole congregation became really quiet as they watched with excitement. She said, "His tumors, are gone; they just disappeared. He had three tumors and each one was the size of a grapefruit."

The next day that couple invited us to lunch. Their friends and family were there, so I taught a short lesson. One of the men got up, came toward me, fell to his knees, and started kissing my shoe. I picked him up and he started touching me, saying, "You are not an angel."

With a chuckle, I said, "No, I'm not an angel."

He said, "My friend was at the service last night, and God healed him of his tumors. He told me to come over and listen to God's message and that God would heal me. As I was listening to the message, God healed me." He said he had cirrhosis of the liver, and the doctors didn't give him much time to live. In this case, this man heard the good news about Christ from his friend, and grabbed hold of it by faith. He had a believing spirit within him when he heard the Good News.

Mark 5:28 (NKJV) says, "If only I may touch His clothes, I shall be made well."

Romans 10:17 (NLT) says, "So faith comes from hearing, that is, hearing the Good News about Christ."

To God be all the glory!

Chapter 15
Believing God's Word During Chaos

In 1991, we were at a revival for three days. On the first night a young lady came up for prayer, and brother Joe prophesized over her and said, "God is showing me that you're going to have a baby and it will be a normal delivery and a healthy baby."

Little did we know that the baby had a ruptured intestine, and the doctors didn't believe the baby would survive. But this young lady believed and grabbed hold of the promises of God. She just kept thanking God for healing her and the baby, and she never wavered in her faith.

On the second day, the same lady came up for prayer and brother Joe spoke the same words to her. Every time she heard those words, she would praise God and dance. *She sure is a happy camper in the Lord,* I thought. Hebrews 13:15 (NASB) says, "Through Him then, let's continually offer up a sacrifice of praise to God, that is, the fruit of lips praising His name."

On the third day, we arrived at the church, and the pastor rushed out, yelling at us in anger. She said, "The church is being sued, and you are being sued for what you said to the young lady who is pregnant." I pulled away because I didn't want to hear the negative confessions.

My brother, Hector, came to where I was and said, "Did you hear what is going on?"

I said, "The devil sure is a liar, isn't he?" 2 Corinthians 2:11 (The Voice) says, "It's my duty to make sure that Satan does not win even a small victory over us, for we don't want to be naïve and then fall prey to his schemes."

My brother, Hector, was a Federal agent with ATF at the time of this testimony, and he gave up a prominent career to serve the Lord.

I continued by saying, "If God said the lady is having a normal delivery and a healthy baby, I believe God's Word more than the lies that the little lying devil is using to create confusion." Hector realized it was a trick of the little lying devil and said, "I stand united with your faith that God is going to give her a normal delivery and a healthy baby."

When the service started, it was dead, dead, dead, I mean dead. We could hear a pin drop. After praise and worship, one of the church staff gave us the microphone, and the doors opened from the back at about the same time. The mother of the pregnant lady walked in and said with excitement, "I want to give a testimony."

I gave her the microphone, and she said, "My daughter was at the doctor's office today. And I want to testify about what happened. The doctor had his lawyers at the office, and they were telling my daughter that no doctor is going to deliver the baby because they were afraid of a lawsuit. They told her she needed to sign a waiver to get a C-section.

While the doctors and lawyers were pressuring her to sign the paper, her water broke and she started having the baby in the office, so the doctor had no choice but to deliver the baby. She had a normal delivery and a healthy baby. The baby came out completely healed."

We never did get sued and neither did the church. The little lying devil always tries to use fear as a tactic to get us to doubt the Word of God. But Proverbs 3:5-6 (NKJV) says, "Trust in the Lord with all your heart, And lean not on your own understanding; In all your ways acknowledge Him, And He shall direct your paths."

King David killing Goliath was one of the greatest moments in history, and Israel got to witness it with their own eyes. Not long after, David went from being a hero to being a criminal in the eyes of King Saul. 1 Samuel 22:1-2 (AMP) says he was on the run and hid in the caves of Adullam:

So David departed from there and escaped to the cave of Adullam; and when his brothers and all his father's house heard about it, they went down there to him. Everyone who was suffering hardship, and everyone who was in debt, and everyone who was discontented gathered to him; and he became captain over them. There were about four hundred men with him.

It looked as though the world was caving in on David and those who followed him.

But no matter how discouraging David's life looked to him, he put God first. He didn't spend his time asking God why King Saul wanted to kill him. He just kept God's promises in his heart and never lost sight of them. He just put his problems in God's hands and trusted Him.

In Psalm 57:7-11, David is exalting and praising God in the cave. David understood that worrying all night wouldn't change the outcome of the next day unless God was involved.

We cannot let problems or chaos control our lives. When we are going through chaos, we need to offer Him praises. Hebrews 13:15 says, "Through Him then, let's continually offer up a sacrifice of praise to God, that is, the fruit of lips praising His name." David knew the truth of Psalm 23:1: "The Lord is my shepherd; I shall not want."

We need to learn to seek God, which means spending time with Him. We need to put our faith in God and praise Him when things look gloomy just like David did. James 1:6-8, (ASV) says, "But let him ask in faith, nothing doubting: for he that doubteth is like the surge of the sea driven by the wind and tossed. For let not that man think that he shall receive anything of the Lord; a doubleminded man, unstable in all his ways."

The little lying devil has a clever way of finding openings into our lives through our emotions and mood swings. At times, the problem we are facing makes us feel there is no way out. We get so discouraged that we let doubts take over our minds. This is the enemy taking steps to defeat us.

But God is merciful to all who call upon Him. We need to learn to praise Him during the tough times. Hebrews 13:15, once again, tells us to "offer up a sacrifice of praise to God."

I praise and glorify the Lord for being merciful!

Chapter 16
No Iris Or Pupil On The Eye

Jeremiah 32:17 (NIV) says, "Ah, Sovereign Lord, you have made the heavens and the earth by your great power and outstretched arm. Nothing is too hard for you."

In 1991 we were in Tamaulipas, Mexico, about an hour outside Reynosa, in a church of about fifteen people. Brother Joe was praying for the sick, and I was just following him. He prayed for a man in a wheelchair, and then he just kept walking.

The man looked at me as if to say, "That's it," and I had compassion on him and asked him if he wanted to be healed. Luke 1:3 (AMP) says, "For with God nothing [is or ever] shall be impossible."

He said, "Yes, I want to be healed."

I said, "Well, get up and walk."

He gave me a look of frustration and shook his head, saying "Yeah, right."

I saw that he had a little faith but needed some help. So, I reached out my hand, and he grabbed it. Then I reached over with my other hand and grabbed his upper arm and yanked him forward out of his wheelchair. I said, "In the name of Jesus, walk or fall."

As he was in the air and going down, he landed on his feet, bracing himself. He started twisting his body back and forth and said, "I am healed."

So I said to him, "Run and start glorifying God, for He is the one who did it."

He ran around inside that church, saying "I am healed! I am healed!"

Once he calmed down, he testified about his miracle, and all the members of that church were praising God. The man said, "I had been run over by a bus and I had a broken spine. They told me I would never walk again. I came to the church to see if they would pray for me and to see if God would heal me. God had mercy over me and healed me."

Hebrews 2:4 (TLB) says, "God always has shown us that these messages are true by signs and wonders and various miracles and by giving certain special abilities from the Holy Spirit to those who believe; yes, God has assigned such gifts to each of us."

The Lord has been gracious to me because I have seen so many miracles like this. I cannot tell you how many people I have seen who were blind or deaf or had cancers or tumors that God has healed instantly. By the power of the Spirit of God, these signs and wonders will accompany those who believe.

Mark 16:20 (TLB) says, "And the disciples went everywhere preaching, and the Lord was with them and confirmed what they said by the miracles that followed their messages." God used miracles like these to build faith.

To God be all the Glory!

A few days after this man was healed, the church was so packed we had to open the windows and doors to accommodate those outside. In the service was a little boy about six years old and blind in one eye. He had no pupil or iris in that eye; it was completely white.

He was in the front row, and I asked him to come to where I was. I hugged him and told him to turn around and face the congregation. I said to the people, "Do you believe God can put a pupil in his eye?"

It was dead silent, and I said, "I believe the God I serve can do this miracle, and in three days he will have a pupil in his eye."

The next night I called the boy up and asked him to face the congregation once again, and I said, "Do you see the brown specs in his eye?" They looked like pen dots, and I knew God was healing him.

The following night I called him up again, and his eye had a brown ring around the center. He was seeing but missing the pupil. God was truly doing a miracle day by day, and the congregation was witnessing it. That night, the congregation was excited, and they started praising and glorifying God for His mighty power.

On the third night I called the boy up again and asked him to face the congregation so they could see his eyes were back to normal. God had put a pupil in his eye, and it was the same as the other eye. God had completely healed him.

Of course, I had my doubting Thomases. They covered his good eye, and they tested the eye that God had healed by asking him, "How many fingers do I have showing?" or "What color is this?" He passed with flying colors.

God had done this miracle slowly in front of the congregation to build their faith. Many times we agree with doubting Thomas, who said, "Except I shall see, I will not believe." But when we make our lips harmonize with the Word of God, it becomes a supernatural force.

To God be all the Glory!

Chapter 17
Praying for Rain

We were preaching and teaching in the rural state of Tamaulipas, Mexico. We were visiting a brother who owned a farm. While he was giving us a tour of his farm, we stopped at one of the fields where he was growing watermelon and cantaloupe. I noticed a man dragging something behind his horse, and, as I pointed to the man, I asked the brother what he was dragging. He said, "It is a Catholic tradition to drag a statue of a saint in the hopes of gaining divine intervention for rain."

With a little chuckle, I asked him, "What happens if it doesn't rain?"

He said, "They will pick another saint and drag him the same way until it rains."

I try not to laugh at people's traditions, but as I was looking at the land, I could tell it hadn't rained in a very long time. So, I said to him, "I guess this tradition isn't working for them. Why don't they just pray to God for rain?"

He said, "May the angels of God listen to the words coming out of your mouth."

A Godly anger came from within me, and I said, "God does listen to my prayers." I looked straight at him and said, "In three days it will rain, so you will know there is a God in heaven."

By this time, the man on the horse showed up. The brother introduced us and told him I had said it would rain in three days. He started saying almost the same thing the other guy had just finished saying. As he was finishing his sentence, I raised my hand, showing three fingers, and said to him, "In three days it will rain. Let us pray." We made a small circle and joined hands in prayer.

After we finished praying, I said to the other man, "My God lives in me, and He will give us the blessings we need."

With respect, he said, "I pray that your God listens to your prayer because we really need the rain."

The pastor and brother Joe came against me by saying, "Why did you say it will rain in three days? What if it doesn't rain? Then what are we going to do here? People will think we aren't men of God."

I said to them, "It is God who provides the blessings, not us. We are supposed to believe His Word. They need to know we serve a living God and not a dead god."

This is where we see whether people are united in the Lord as one, and at the same time, we see how much faith they really have. Brother Joe had the most beautiful ministry I had ever seen, but my portion of faith was greater than his.

When it comes to the gifts of the Holy Spirit, we are given a different measure. When acting in faith, we have to stand on the Word for His promises.

My daughter was in college and wanted extra money, so I told her to fill out a scholarship application. She had to complete specific requirements to have any chance of receiving that scholarship. One of these requirements was to write an essay. Once she completed all the requirements, she sent in her application. There was no way for her to change what she had sent in; she just had to wait for a response. Later, she received a response telling her she had been granted the scholarship.

Those men we visited on the farm wanted rain. One of the requirements for receiving the rain was to study the Word to see what God's promises are. Just like writing an essay to receive a scholarship, we have to believe God and do what He says to receive His blessings. This is faith; the action is believing it will rain. When we prayed for rain, we sent our mail to God and waited for His response.

We have to treat spiritual mail the same way we treat natural mail. When we mail something in the natural, it goes on its way until it gets to its destination, and nothing stops it. And we cannot change or take back what we have sent. Spiritual mail, even when it's mailed out and heading toward its destination, we still can take it back by speaking doubt or unbelief. I don't believe God has heard us and we have to pray for rain again. You have to let it get to its destination which is God's throne, because when you speak doubt, you are replanting instead of watering. We have to keep the soil moist so it takes root.

We have to hold fast to our confession in the face of all contrary evidence. Hebrews 4:14 (ASV) says, "...Jesus the Son of God, let us hold fast our confession." Hebrews 10:23 (ASV) continues with, "Let us seize and hold tightly the confession of our hope without wavering, for He who promised is reliable and trustworthy and faithful to His word." Christ is the mediator of our promises. When we hold fast to what we pray for and waver not, He is faithful to His Word.

The words I had spoken, "It will rain in three days," had already gone forth. I had to stand on the Word of God and start thanking Him for the rain. Hebrews 11:1 (NKJV) says, "Now faith is the substance of things hoped for, the evidence of things not seen." I had to put my spiritual senses to work.

The spiritual senses are the same as the five natural senses, except they are invisible because they are in the spiritual realm. Spiritual blessings are invisible, and we have to convert the invisible to visible by faith. This sounds, looks, and feels like a lie, but God requires it.

In this world we see through natural sight and not spiritual sight. 2 Kings 6:16-17 (NLT) says, "Don't be afraid! Elisha told him. For there are more on our side than on theirs! Then Elisha prayed, O Lord, open his eyes and let him see! The Lord opened the young man's eyes, and when he looked up, he saw that the hillside around Elisha was filled with horses and chariots of fire."

2 Corinthians 4:18 (AMP) says, "So we look not at the things which are seen, but at the things which are unseen; for the things which are visible are temporal [just brief and fleeting], but the things which are invisible are everlasting and imperishable."

We have to step out of the natural-sense realm and into the spiritual-sense realm. Instead of listening or accepting what Satan is offering, we must be working with God, who heals us and gives us His blessings by His Word.

The next day I started asking the people if they could see the clouds coming. They would look up into the sky and not see one cloud. But I was seeing the invisible clouds in the sky. They would shake their heads no and keep looking at the sky to see if they could see any clouds. I just kept telling them, "I am seeing the clouds coming, and it is going to rain." They would smile at me and shake their heads because they seemed to think I was a nut. But I said the same thing to every person I saw that morning.

In the afternoon I started asking them if they could hear the rumble of the thunder. They would look at the sky and give me a strange look because there was still not a cloud to be seen. But I was hearing the invisible thunder. So, I kept telling them, "I am hearing the thunder, and it is going to rain." They would shake their heads no and keep looking at the sky to see if they could hear any thunder or see any clouds. Once again, they would smile at me and shake their heads. But I said the same thing to every person I saw that afternoon.

The second day I asked them if they could smell the rain. "Hmm, it smells so good," I would say, "and everything smells wet. Can you smell it?" At first, they would try to smell the rain, but after a couple of sniffs they would give up. But I smelled the invisible rain and told them it was raining. Once again, they just shook their heads and smiled at me. But I did this with everyone I saw that morning.

In the afternoon I started asking them if they could feel the rain. I would have my hands extended, touching and feeling the invisible rain falling into my hands. I would tell them, "Feel it; it is rain." I would extend my arms and shake them so they could feel the invisible rain. All this time, there wasn't a cloud in the sky, and the people just kept looking at me as though I had missing marbles in my head.

Most of the third day, I stayed in my room and prayed. As I was meditating on the Word of God, the scripture that came to mind was where Elijah prayed for rain. As I was pondering this, I saw how good God was when He sent a cloud to Elijah. 1 Kings 18:44 (ESV) says, "Behold, a little cloud like a man's hand is rising from the sea." My prayer to the Lord that day was, "Please put a small cloud in the sky to help build the people's faith."

That afternoon I saw a few clouds. I said to the people as I pointed toward the clouds, "You see it? Here it comes. It is going to rain." Now I could see they had more faith because they were actually seeing some clouds. They weren't shaking their heads at me anymore.

Late in the afternoon, the clouds started getting thicker, and all the people started saying it was going to rain. That night it rained so much, the people were so happy, and they no longer saw me as a nut. They saw I had a connection with God, and this made it easy to teach them the things of God.

From that day forward, I started teaching that God lives in us:

- Luke 17:21 (GNT) says, "...because the Kingdom of God is within you."
- 1 Corinthians 12:27 (NIV) says, "Now you are the body of Christ, and each one of you is a part of it."
- 1 Corinthians 6:17 (AMP) says, "But the one who is united and joined to the Lord is one spirit with Him."
- 1 Corinthians 2:16 (AMP) says, "For who has known the mind and purposes of the Lord, so as to instruct Him? But we have the mind of Christ [to be guided by His thoughts and purposes]."
- Galatians 2:20 (NKJV) says, "I have been crucified with Christ; it is no longer I who live, but Christ lives in me...."

To paraphrase these five scriptures, the kingdom of God is within us, and we are the body of Christ. We are united and joined to the Lord in one spirit with Him. We have the mind of Christ, which means we are guided by His thoughts. It is no longer we who live but Christ who lives in us.

We have to know who we are in Christ. Faith lifts the floodgates and lets the flow go through. We are to think, speak, and act on our faith until the promise is fulfilled. Faith without action is dead faith.

I praise and glorify the Lord for all His goodness toward us!

Chapter 18
Authority Over Demons

Luke 7:7-8 (NASB) says, "For I also am a man placed under authority, with soldiers under myself; and I say to this one, 'Go!' and he goes, and to another, 'Come!' and he comes, and to my slave, 'Do this!' and he does it."

The centurion in this scripture is saying, "I have authority from a higher power, which comes from Caesar." If the centurion gave an order to the soldier, he would obey without questioning him. The centurion recognized that Jesus Christ had authority over sickness and that He didn't have to be next to the sick person to heal them. He only had to say the word, and sickness obeyed.

If a policeman knocks on your door, he might say, "Open in the name of the law." What law? The law that was put in place by a higher power, which is the state. The state is the one that gave him a badge with the authority to enforce the law.

All authority comes to us from a higher power. It flows from above. We must be under Christ's authority to have power over sickness, evil spirits, and demons. Our authority is linked to our obedience in Christ. This means not only knowing Him, but also spending time with Him, having an intimate relationship with Him. It means loving Him with all our soul, putting Him first above all things.

Christ gave us the pattern, "the Father and I are one." Christ is our higher power; we are the body of Christ, united as one in Him:

- Galatians 2:20 (AMP) says, "it is no longer I who live, but Christ lives in me."
- 1 Corinthians 12:27 (NIV) says, "Now you are the body of Christ, and each one of you is a part of it."
- 1 Corinthians 6:17 (AMP) says, "But the one who is united and joined to the Lord is one spirit with Him."
- And Luke 17:20 (GNT) says, "…because the Kingdom of God is within you."

Christ lives in me and I in Him; we are one. Always pay attention to what Christ is saying in the scriptures. He gives us the pattern for what we are supposed to do. In Matthew 28:18-20 (NLT):

> Jesus came and told his disciples, 'I have been given all authority in heaven and on earth. Therefore, go and make disciples of all the nations, baptizing them in the name of the Father and the Son and the Holy Spirit. Teach these new disciples to

obey all the commands I have given you. And be sure of this: I am with you always, even to the end of the age.'

Christ is saying, "All authority is given to me." This means everything is subject to Him. He wants us to execute His authority by obeying His Word, His commandments, and His Will. The only way to gain this kind of authority with power is to put in lots of time with the Lord by reading, praying, meditating, fasting, and testifying. This doesn't mean ten minutes; this means hours with Him.

When we get close to the Lord, we carry this authority and can cast out any demon we come across. As I traveled through Mexico, I fasted three to five days per week. I spent six to eight hours a day reading, meditating, and praying in His presence. I'm not trying to exalt myself, but we have to spend lots of time with the Lord to see this kind of power. Satan tries to keep us from learning the truth of the authority we have in Christ.

In 1991, we were in a church in Reynosa, Mexico, where the presence of the Lord was very strong. The church was so packed it was going to take us a long time to pray for all the people. So brother Joe, brother Hector, and I decided to line up twenty in front of us. As we lifted our hands and prayed, the people were slain by the Holy Spirit. We never touched them. They would hit the ground unconscious and stay that way for a while. We had to form another line, and they went down the same way. Many gave their testimony that night of how the Lord had healed them.

At the end of the service they brought in a woman. Six men carried her over their heads, and she was fighting them. They came straight to us. They put her down and she began speaking in a man's voice, and she was mad. One of the men next to me said the woman was demon possessed. The woman looked confused. She was just looking from side to side, muttering words.

In the man's voice, she said, "You have no power over me" and ripped her clothes off, like a professional wrestler rips his shirt off on TV. He said that he owned her, that he was going to stay in her, and that we couldn't do anything about it.

I looked at that demon-possessed woman and said, "In the name of Jesus I bind you. Hush; do not speak." She continued moving her head from side to side. Only this time she was trying to talk but could not. I asked one of the men who had brought her in, "What is her name?" He said her name was Louisa.

I spoke to the demon-possessed woman again and commanded Louisa's spirit to come forth. As she was moving around, Louisa started speaking with her own voice, crying "Please help me. I asked her if she wanted to be delivered from this demon, and she said, "Yes, please set me free from this demon; please help me."

I quoted scriptures of power. The first was 1 Corinthians 15:27 (NLT): "For the Scriptures say, 'God has put all things under his authority….'"

The second was Ephesians 1:19-22 (NLT): "Now he is far above any ruler or authority or power or leader or anything else—not only in this world but also in the world to come. God has put all things under the authority of Christ and has made him head over all things for the benefit of the church."

I said to the demon, "It is written in the Word of God. You have no power over this woman." I pointed my finger at her and said, "In the name of Jesus, who has all authority and power, I command you to come out of her right now."

Her body was swaying back and forth, and the demon came out of her. She fell to the ground as though she had no strength in her. She had been delivered and made whole. They covered her with a blanket, and as she started gaining her strength, she started crying and saying, "Thank you."

Matthew 17:18-19, 21 (KJV) says:

And Jesus rebuked the devil; and he departed out of him: and the child was cured from that very hour. Then came the disciples to Jesus apart, and said, "Why could not we cast him out?" His disciples could not cast out this demon and Jesus give the answer to why.... "Howbeit this kind goeth not out but by prayer and fasting."

To God be all the Glory!

When we trust God's power, we draw strength from Him. Ephesians 6:12 (NLT) says, "For we are not fighting against flesh-and-blood enemies, but against evil rulers and authorities of the unseen world, against mighty powers in this dark world, and against evil spirits in the heavenly places."

Why would God give us authority to act for Him if we spend no time with Him? The demons recognize valid authority, and they fear God. James 4:7-8 (AMP) instructs us,

"So submit to the authority of God. Resist the devil stand firm against him and he will flee from you. Come close to God with a contrite heart and He will come close to you.…"

We have the victory over any demonic force. We just have to exercise that authority in Christ. If we want to cast out a demon, we need to be sure we are spending time with God in the Word and that we are fasting and praying so we can have the authority to cast out the demon. That way, we don't end up like the seven sons of Sceva the priest in Acts 19:13-16, who were trying to cast out evil spirits, and one of them leaped on them and beat them.

To God be all the Glory!

Chapter 19
Angel of God in the Church Service

We were having a three-day revival and the first night the Lord performed so many miracles, which brought in so many sick people. That same night a woman who was blind came up for prayer. I said, playing around, "Grandma, what do you need?"

She replied, "For God to heal me."

"What are you sick of?" I asked.

She said, "I have been blind for fifteen years, and I would love to see with my eyes again."

I hugged her and said, "Let us pray for your eyes."

I put one hand over each of her eyes and prayed, "Lord, heal her eyes, and let her see clearly again. In the name of Jesus, I rebuke that spirit of blindness."

I took my hands off her eyes, and said, "What do you see?"

She said, "I see clearly with my left eye, but my right eye is still blurry."

I remembered what Mark 8:24 (AMP) said about the blind man Jesus prayed for. After praying for him, He asked him, "What do you see?"

"And he looked up and said, 'I see people, but [they look] like trees, walking around.'

In verse 25 (AMP), "Then again Jesus laid His hands on his eyes; and the man stared intently and [his sight] was [completely] restored, and he *began* to see everything clearly."

I said to the elderly woman, "Let us pray again," and I covered the eye that needed complete healing and prayed the same prayer. She opened her eyes and started crying. She said, "I am seeing clearly with both eyes." I told her to praise and glorify God for healing her.

That night we saw so many healings it would be hard to write them all.

The second night the church was packed. When we started praying for the sick, the woman I called "Grandma" came up to me and said, "Can you pray for my friends? I have been testifying about how the Lord healed me last night, and I brought my friends so they may receive their healing."

She brought three elderly women who were also blind. I saw that they had faith to be healed, so I prayed for each of them, and God healed all of them.

To God be all the Glory!

That same night we prayed for a married couple who wanted to receive the baptism of the Holy Spirit. They both started speaking in tongues, praise God. Acts 19:6 (NKJV) says, "And when Paul had laid hands on them, the Holy Spirit came upon them, and they spoke with tongues and prophesied."

On the third day, we were driving to the church to pray, and there was an old man who said "God sent me here. The Lord showed me this church, which had two doves in front of the building, and said I would find three men." When he saw us, he said, "You're the ones I'm looking for. I was at the entrance of heaven, and the Lord told me to go back and give these three men a message."

He started telling each of us our secret prayers to God that only He would know. He took each of us aside and gave us our special message. He told me something that was prophesied to me some time back, and he also said I would be married the following year. He even described the woman who would become my wife.

Everything came to pass as he said. After he visited with each of us, we were all asking the same thing: is this an angel of God? Hebrews 13:2 (NLT) says, "Don't forget to show hospitality to strangers, for some who have done this have entertained angels without realizing it!"

That night we had a service we called "the Pool of Bethesda." The story is found in John 5. We used a small plastic pool and added about three inches of water, just enough to wet the feet. The older man we met that day said to me, "I can play any instrument," and he picked up the guitar and started playing and singing. He played serval songs, and I could feel the strong presence of the Lord.

Once again, the church was packed and after the praise

and worship we said to the crowd, If any of you are sick or need anything from the Lord, step into the pool and let God do the miracle." John 5:2-4 (NKJV) says:

"Now there is in Jerusalem by the Sheep Gate a pool, which is called in Hebrew, Bethesda, having five porches. In these lay a great multitude of sick people, blind, lame, paralyzed, waiting for the moving of the water. For an angel went down at a certain time into the pool and stirred up the water; then whoever stepped in first, after the stirring of the water, was made well of whatever disease he had."

It felt as though the angel of God was stirring the water in the pool, and everyone who stepped into the pool was being healed, whether spiritually or physically.

Remember the couple who spoke in tongues the night before they brought their friends to receive the baptism of the Holy Spirit? We asked them to step into the pool and let God do the miracle. As soon as they stepped into the pool, they started praising and glorifying God, and they were speaking in tongues.

That night we went to visit an older couple who was too sick to make it to the service. Then we had a late dinner, and the older man asked us if we would drop him off at the bus station. It was after midnight, and he didn't want to stay with us. We aren't in a big city, so the bus station was a small building, and the man would have to wait outside for the bus.

After we dropped him off, we drove around the block and decided to go back for him, but he was gone. We searched for him, but we couldn't find him. The bus stop was just an open field; we were in the middle of nowhere. So where did he go? We knew for certain that an angel of God was in our midst.

We never know if we are entertaining an angel of the Lord. By showing warm, generous hospitality to our brothers and sisters in Christ, we are being faithful and obedient to the Lord's will.

To God be all the Glory!

By Alex Valenzuela

Chapter 20
Obeyed and Went

Hebrews 11:8 (NLT) says, "It was by faith that Abraham obeyed, when God called him to leave home and go to another land that God would give him as his inheritance. He went without knowing where he was going."

How many of us would listen to the call of God if He told us to go someplace without telling us where we were going? Abraham traveled 1500 miles without knowing where he was going. The life of faith is a life of taking steps forward in obedience.

We were preaching in Tamaulipas, Mexico in 1991. We were in a city called Progresso, and brother Joe had a dream. The next day he shared his dream with the pastor and me, and the pastor said, "What you just described is my hometown in the state of Hidalgo about a fourteen-hour drive from here."

God put it in our spirit to go to Hidalgo. Ephesians 2:10 (NIV) says, "For we are God's handiwork, created in Christ Jesus to do good works, which God prepared in advance for us to do." The pastor decided to go on our adventure. We didn't know what awaited us there or how the people were going to receive us. We just trusted God's call and went by faith.

When we arrived in Hidalgo, we stayed in a city called Huehuetla. From there we visited the surrounding villages. The pastor informed us as we went into the villages that most of the people didn't speak Spanish. They spoke a dialect language called Nahuatl of the Aztec empire. But we discovered the younger generation did speak Spanish.

The people were so hungry for the Word of God, and the Lord was moving in healing, deliverance, and salvation. Many people would be outside our hut at about five or six in the morning, waiting for us to get up so we could join them for breakfast and share the Word of God.

I love to drink coffee in the morning, and they would make me a fresh pot from beans they had grown themselves. They would grind the beans and throw them into a pot of boiling water. They didn't filter the coffee, so it was raw and strong. The first time I drank it, I could see all the coffee grounds floating in my cup. Psalm 34:1 (NKJV) says, "I will bless the Lord at all times; His praise shall continually be in my mouth."

This area was tropical, and I loved all the different fruits they had for me to eat. I had fresh orange juice whenever I wanted it.

The night service would end around ten or eleven. After a few nights, we started noticing more and more people coming to the service. We found out that many of them lived one or two hours away. So, we decided to start feeding the people after the service.

This was one of the poorest areas I had ever been in, so we used whatever money we had saved to feed them. It was like traveling back in time to the mid-1800s. The restroom was either a small outhouse made of bamboo sticks or two cinder blocks that we sat on, with a tarp around the area to block the view.

The outhouse I used was the one with the two cinder blocks with a tarp. I was sitting on the cinder blocks, and I know for a fact that God has a sense of humor because there was no wind blowing. Out of nowhere a soft wind started blowing and picked up the tarp. I could see all the brothers and sisters looking my way. I waved my hand at them to see if they could see me, and they smiled and waved back at me. One guy even gave me the thumbs up, so I guess I was doing it right.

They didn't want me to take my bath in the river because I was a man of God, and they didn't want people to see me naked. The irony is, the washroom where I took my bath was also made of bamboo sticks, and each stick had a four-inch gap so they could still see me taking a bath.

One of the young men would ride his donkey in and bring me five gallons of water every day. I called it my Navy shower, also known as the combat shower. Wet the whole body with the water, lather up with soap and shampoo, and then rinse off.

We stayed about two months, but after that, we had other obligations. I prayed that God would send me back at a later time, which He did.

To God be all the Glory!

We are to be more like Abraham, obeying the call and going to the unknown. It amazes me that Abraham left everything he knew when he was seventy-five years old. Just imagine leaving all your friends and family behind, and when people ask you where you're going, you tell them, "I really don't know; God just told me to travel south."

"How are you going to support yourself and provide for your family?" they will ask.

"I don't know. I am just obeying Him at His Word. Since it is God telling me to go, I am sure He will provide for me and my family as I go forward."

Proverbs 20:24 (TLB) says, "Since the Lord is directing our steps, why try to understand everything that happens along the way?"

I can only imagine what people were saying to him. "Are you sure it is God calling you? I don't know if you're really hearing God because you and your wife are too old to be traveling. Are you sure you want to make your wife suffer on this journey?"

Matthew 6:31-32 (GNT) says, "So do not start worrying: 'Where will my food come from? or my drink? or my clothes?' (These are the things the pagans are always concerned about.) Your Father in heaven knows that you need all these things."

We are called to go out and preach and teach the Good News regardless of our age.

I praise and glorify God for guiding us!

Chapter 21
Raising The Dead

In 1991, I saw two men and one child raised from the dead. We were in the jungles of Mexico and God was moving in miracles. Mark 16:20 (AMP) says, "And they went out and preached everywhere, while the Lord was working with them and confirming the word by the signs that followed."

People were coming from everywhere up to two hours away. We started feeding the people at about 10 p.m. and a young lady asked for prayer for her son. So, we laid hands on the child and prayed. Brother Joe told her to take the child home and feed him rice water, and she did. The next day she asked us to visit her.

It was a thirty-minute walk to her house, and she looked so happy when she saw us approaching. She was looking at us with the same kind of love that a woman and a man show one another when they are truly in love.

We had an interpreter with us who spoke mostly Nahuatl, the language of the Aztec empire. She gave us her testimony and said her child had died two days ago. She added that many of her neighbors had gone to us for prayer and were healed. They kept telling me, "God is doing miracles through them; go and see them. Have them lay hands on your child and see if God will bring him back to life."

"The more I heard what God was doing," she said, "the more I started to believe that God could do the impossible. I couldn't accept my son's death because my baby had done no wrong. I started believing God with all my heart that when they touched my son, he would come back to life."

The woman continued to testify, "That night I took him to the service and after the service, I asked for prayer. When you all prayed for him and said, 'Make him rice water when you get home and feed him, I did as I was commanded. After making the rice water, I went to my dead child and put the bottle in his mouth to feed him, and he started gasping for air.'"

Now if we had known the baby was dead, we probably would have said something different to her because doubt and fear would have crept into our spirits. But 2 Kings 4:27 (NKJV) says, "But the man of God said, Let her alone; for her soul is in deep distress, and the Lord has hidden it from me, and has not told me." Sometimes God has to hide information so we will not waver with doubt.

I saw the child again in 1995 and he was a healthy boy.

Praise God; all the Glory is His!

2 Kings 4:8-37 tells a story about Elisha and a dead child. I will paraphrase the story here, but please read it on your own to understand what was happening.

In Shunem, a rich woman said to her husband, "Let's build a small room for the man of God."

Every time Elisha went to Shunem he would stay there. He asked his servant, Gehazi, "What can I do for this woman who is so kind to us?"

His servant said, "She doesn't have a child."

Elisha prayed that she would have a child, and the following year she did. When the child was old enough to work, he decided to work with his father. While he was working, the boy got sick, so his father sent him home to his mother. The boy died in his mother's lap.

She couldn't accept his death, so she told her husband to have a servant saddle a donkey because she was going to see the man of God. The husband asked her if everything was all right. She said, "It is well," continuing to act in faith. She wasn't going to speak death upon her child.

While she was on her way to see the man of God, Elisha saw her from a distance and sent Gehazi to meet her. When he caught up to her, he asked "Is it well with your family?"

Once again, she said, "All is well," because she wasn't going to speak death. Here we see that she isn't letting a lie come between the promises of God and her family. 2 Kings 4:27 (NKJV) says, "But the man of God said, Let her alone; for her soul is in deep distress, and the Lord has hidden it from me, and has not told me."

Elisha told Gehazi to lay his staff on the child's face, but the child didn't awaken. So he ran back to meet Elisha and told him what had happened, and Elisha ran back to the house. Here we see that God had to hide from Elisha the fact that the child was dead because if he would have known, he would have probably started thinking, *What am I going to do with a dead child? Oh I hope God hears my prayer.*

Verses 32-33 (NKJV) say, "When Elisha came into the house, there was the child, lying dead on his bed. He went in therefore, shut the door behind the two of them, and prayed to the Lord."

In verse 35, Elisha was praying for the child: "He returned and walked back and forth in the house, and again went up and stretched himself out on him; then the child sneezed seven times, and the child opened his eyes." God answered Elisha's prayer and healed the child. I praise and glorify the Lord for He is good to us.

The second person I saw raised from the dead that year was a pastor. We had been preaching at his church. One day we arrived at the church and the pastor was on the ground. We shook him but he didn't move. He was dead. So we called for the ambulance. The paramedics arrived and said upon examining him that he had died of a heart attack. As I stood there, I shook my head and said, "It is a lie."

They had him on the stretcher and were taking him toward the ambulance. I walked to the stretcher, put my hands on the pastor, and commanded his spirit to come back. To my surprise, he started gasping for air. He sat up, he was breathing; he was alive. Luke 7:14-15 (AMP) says, "And He came up and touched the bier [on which the body rested], and the pallbearers stood still. And He said, Young man, I say to you, arise [from death]! The man who was dead sat up and began to speak. And Jesus gave him back to his mother." God had brought the pastor back from the dead.

To God be all the Glory!

The third person I saw raised from the dead in 1991 was brother Joe, the one I had been learning from. The church service had just finished, and brother Joe looked exhausted. He walked to the bench and sat down. When I looked toward him, I saw him feeling around his chest, and then he passed out. I checked on him, but he wasn't moving. The pastor, who was also a paramedic, checked him out, as well, and said, "He is dead."

I pushed people out of the way, put my hands on him, and commanded his spirit to come back. His spirit returned to his body and he started gasping for air.

Later that night he told me he was out of his body when he died, and he could see all the people praying over him. He said, "I saw you pushing the crowd away and putting your hands on me, commanding my spirit to come back. Then I found myself back in my body."

Paul said about a brother in the Lord in Philippians 2:27 (TLB), "And he surely was; in fact, he almost died. But God had mercy on him and on me, too, not allowing me to have this sorrow on top of everything else." The Lord had mercy on me that day. I would have had a tough time accepting his death, and I was glad God noticed that.

To God be all the Glory!

Chapter 22
With God All Things Are Possible

Luke 18:27 (NKJV) says, "But He said, "The things which are impossible with men are possible with God."

1 Peter 1:8-9 (GNT) says, "You love him, although you have not seen him, and you believe in him, although you do not now see him. So you rejoice with a great and glorious joy which words cannot express, because you are receiving the salvation of your souls, which is the purpose of your faith in him."

When I was in Mexico in 1991, there was a woman who was full of cancer and dying in the jungle of Hildago. Her friends told her there were some men preaching the Word of God and many of the people going to them were being healed of their sicknesses. So, her friends encouraged her to come see us and let us pray for her so that God would heal her.

In Luke 5:17-26, there was a paralyzed man whose friends carried him on a stretcher to Jesus. There was a large crowd there, but they were determined to get their friend in front of Jesus so that he would be healed. So they made a hole in the roof and lowered the paralyzed man down. After Jesus saw their faith, He healed him. Luke 5:25 (NLT) says, "And immediately, as everyone watched, the man jumped up, picked up his mat, and went home praising God."

The woman decided to go with her friends, and as she was traveling, she repeatedly fainted and fell to the ground. Her friends would fan air to her face and encourage her, and then she would get up and travel again. She was in so much pain, but she kept telling her friends, "I need to keep going. When they pray for me, I am going to be healed."

After they had been traveling awhile, her friends said, "It's not far from here; let's keep going." That night she made it to the service, and she heard the message, "With God all things are possible."

She listened to the message and said, "God can save my soul and heal my body at the same time." As we were praying for the sick, she came up, raised her arms, accepted Jesus Christ as her Savior, and said to Him, "I will serve you and follow all your ways."

She started jumping up and down in joy. When she stopped jumping, she realized she was completely healed; the cancer was gone. She said, "I don't know where it went, but I'm completely healed."

That night she testified about her journey with her friends and how God had healed her. With God all things are possible.

To God be all the Glory!

That same year, we were having a revival by Reynosa, Mexico, and encountered a man with rheumatoid arthritis. I told him that God could heal his condition. He just shook his head from side to side and said, "yeah." He had no faith at all, but I still invited him to the revival we were having at his village. For the next three nights, he came to the revival but never came for prayer. Once the revival ended, we left for Hildago.

His family kept in touch with some of the people who followed us. His family saw his faith in God starting to grow because he would tell them, "If those men of God would pray for me, I would be healed." So his parents decided to sell what they could and scrape up enough money to send him to us. At that point, we were about ten hours away from their village.

They couldn't scrape up enough money for a round trip. They said that when God heals him, he can hitchhike home. They paid a man to take him to us, and that man just left him close to the place where we were having services.

That night the young man was listening to the message, "With God all things are possible," and he said to himself, "Tonight is my night to be healed." He said, "I believe in God, I believe in Jesus Christ, and I believe all things are possible with God. I believe He is the Son of God, I believe He died for my sins, and I believe He sits on the right side of the Father in heaven. I believe he is going to heal me tonight."

Then he came crawling to the altar for prayer, having faith that God would heal him. I picked him up and started hugging him. First we prayed for his salvation, and after he accepted Jesus Christ as his Savior, tears came running down his eyes.

Then he said, "Pray for me to be healed. I believe God is

going to heal me tonight. He couldn't stretch his arms out, and he couldn't walk without falling. He was hunched over with this crippling disease, but that night he believed with God all things are possible.

We prayed for him, and his bones started crackling. I shook him and heard more crackling. I put him down and said to him, "Keep moving your hands, arms, and legs, and start twisting your hips." He was crackling so much that when it stopped, he stood in front of me completely healed.

This young man's faith was similar to the woman who had been constantly bleeding for twelve years. Her story is found in Mark 5:25-34. She kept saying "If I can just touch his robe, I will be healed," just like the young man was saying, "When they pray for me, I am going to be healed."

After he was healed, a friend of mine who was going toward Reynosa gave him a ride home.

With God all things are possible.

To God be all the Glory!

By Alex Valenzuela

Chapter 23
Ending Evangelism and Starting a New Ministry

Matthew 28:18-20 (NIV) says, "Then Jesus came to them and said, "All authority in heaven and on earth has been given to me. Therefore go and make disciples of all nations, baptizing them in the name of the Father and of the Son and of the Holy Spirit, and teaching them to obey everything I have commanded you. And surely, I am with you always, to the very end of the age."

And Luke 10:2 (NIV) says, "He told them, The harvest is plentiful, but the workers are few. Ask the Lord of the harvest, therefore, to send out workers into his harvest field."

In December of 1991, we were visiting brother Manuel and his family in Casa Grandes Chihuahua, Mexico. We had been there eleven months earlier and had prayed that God would heal his wife's barrenness. God listened to our prayer, and she got pregnant and had a baby girl. When we arrived, the baby was two months old.

Brother Joe went back to the United States, and I stayed in Mexico. He was supposed to wire me some money when I was ready to go home, but for some reason, I never received the money, so I was stranded for three months with a nickel in my pocket. The Lord had shown me that it was His will for me to be there and for me to stay put. I was preaching in some of the churches there, and many of the people started bringing me dry goods, like coffee, sugar, flour, and beans.

Every day brother Manuel and I went hunting with a BB gun, and we never missed when we shot it. We would kill three or four quails, three or four doves, three or four cottontail rabbits every day for three months. We would invite different people to come eat with us because there was so much food. It was winter, and it had snowed, which made it harder for me to leave Mexico, but God just kept providing and we never lacked. 1 Kings 17 tells us that God fed Elijah by ravens.

There is nothing hard for God. All He wants is for us to have faith in Him and to take the step of action by believing His Word. Instead of listening to Satan and looking at our situation, we must be working with God, who heals and protects us by His Word. We must grab hold of His promises, keep them deep within our souls, and not let go. Faith is having complete confidence in God, knowing we can depend on Him to do what He says He will do.

I praise and glorify God for watching over us!

By Alex Valenzuela

In March of 1992, after being snowed in in Mexico, the Lord told me to go to Hobbs, New Mexico. He did not tell me why I was going; He just said "go." I called brother Hector to let him know the Lord was sending me to Hobbs. He was so happy by the news that he said, "Brother, I have to preach in Monahan, Texas, and I will take you there."

The Lord showed me in my spirit to go and see my cousin that I had not seen since childhood. She lived in Hobbs. When I found her, she said "The Lord has blessed me with a new home with an in-law house in the back." The Lord showed her that I was coming and to welcome me into her home.

Well, to make a long story short, I found out my old girlfriend from high school was working at one of the banks. I went to visit her, and we hit it off again. We visited a church, and they had a guest speaker from Houston, Texas, and he called both of us to the front. He said, "I have a prophecy from God for you." The prophecy that was given to me was a similar one that was given to me in Mexico.

When he turned to my soon-to-be-wife, he said, "My daughter, I have brought him to you from far away. Yes, I have seen your tears, and I have brought him to you from far away." That is when I realize that God had brought me to get married. Remember the angel in the service that gave me words, he said, "You will be married next year." God was giving me a good wife who was willing to serve God with all her heart. Our spirits were united as one to serve the Lord in whatever He called us to do. She became my right-hand supporter to go and win souls for the Lord.

To God be all the Glory!

By Alex Valenzuela

Chapter 24
Call To The Mission Field

In 1994 the Lord spoke to me while I was driving and told me to go back to Hidalgo, but I didn't want to go. I had a family, and no one was financially supporting me. Within days the spirit of the Lord put within my spirit a great burning love for the people in Hidalgo, Mexico. I had a desire to go and witness over there. Jeremiah 20:9 (GNT) says, "...then your message is like a fire burning deep within me...." So, I decided to just step out in faith and go. I asked the Lord how to go about it. I didn't speak the language, and I didn't have the funds to support my family or even get there.

My pastor kept asking me whether I was really hearing from God. He kept saying, "You have a family. You just cannot leave them behind with no support." He even threw scripture at me, like 1 Timothy 5:8 (GNT): "But if any do not take care of their relatives, especially the members of their own family, they have denied the faith and are worse than an unbeliever."

I tried to assure him that it was the Lord calling me to go and that all would be well with my family and me. Ephesians 2:10 (NIV) says, "For we are God's handiwork, created in Christ Jesus to do good works, which God prepared in advance for us to do." The Lord also comforted me so that I wouldn't be worried about my family lacking anything.

Then He gave me a dream and showed me a pastor who spoke the language and who was going to be helping me in the ministry. The Lord kept giving me dreams of the jungle and the mountains where I was going. He showed me the work I would be doing there, though it didn't make sense at the time.

The pastor in my dreams was the same guy who went with us in 1991, and he didn't have a phone, so I had to depend on God to give him the same dream or vision. Numbers 12:6 (KJV) says, "And he said, Hear now my words: If there be a prophet among you, I the Lord will make myself known unto him in a vision, and will speak unto him in a dream."

Believe it or not, I never received any kind of support from any church. God had to send people to me to support not only my trip, but my family and the pastor's family that was going with me.

Well, I just showed up at his house and knocked. When he opened the door, I could tell he was excited to see me, and he told me he was ready to go. He pointed toward his duffle bag and said, "The Lord showed me a dream that you were coming and told me to go with you. He told me that I would be your interpreter and that I would be with you as long as you needed me."

When God calls us to go on a mission for Him, He will make it happen. He doesn't need ATT or Verizon. He still uses dreams and visions to communicate.

I worked in Hidalgo for several years. I would spend four to six weeks there and then go home to my family for three to four months so I could work to meet their needs. Then I would go back to Mexico.

As I traveled through the jungle, the Lord would remind me of the dreams that made no sense to me at the time He gave them to me. One time I dreamed about a lady who was in a wheelchair because she had a broken back. I met her one day while I was walking, and I asked her if I could pray a blessing for her. She said that I could, so I laid my hands on her and prayed for her healing. God did an instant miracle, and she got up and started walking. She was completely healed.

As I walked, God would remind me of the dream, and, with a smile on my face, I would cherish the moment. God gave me grace with the people there and He protected me. This isn't a place I would have wanted to be if God hadn't called me. There was no electricity, no running water, and no roads. This means no air conditioning, no indoor toilet or shower, and mosquitoes all around me. They would bring me five gallons of water on a donkey so I could take a bath.

Most of the missions we started were thirty minutes to two hours away, which meant I had to walk through the jungle. On the day I was going home I went to the nearest city, which was Huehuetla. I could go to a bank and use my debit card to get money from the ATM. To my surprise, the day I went, the ATM didn't give me any money. It just kept giving me an error message. It was on a Saturday, and the bank was closed so I couldn't talk to anybody, and I didn't have a cent on me.

I headed toward the bus station and there were about a hundred people from different missions to see me off. When I am going through something like this, the little lying devil never fails to mess with my mind. All I could hear was, "How are you going to get home? You don't have any money. How are you going to buy your bus ticket?"

I have always trusted my Lord, and He has always made a way for me. While I was heading toward the bus station, I had to put faith in action to receive my blessings. I decided to get my bus ticket. So, I waited in line, and when it was my turn at the counter, I ordered my ticket to Reynosa. The man at the counter told me how many pesos it would cost. Right at that moment, a brother in the Lord said, "I want to be a blessing to you. I want to pay for the ticket," and he paid. So, I got my ticket and walked toward the bus.

Now when the bus was boarding, all the Christians followed me. The bus driver looked so happy, probably because he thought we were all getting on. After hugging them, I got on the bus, and they were crying because they were sad to see me go. The bus driver said, "You're the only one," and I shook my head yes.

At that moment I understood what Paul experienced in Acts 21:5 (GNT) while he was getting on the ship in

Tyre: "while all of the disciples, with their wives and children, escorted us on our way until we were outside the city. After kneeling down on the beach and praying, we told one another goodbye."

That burning desire the Lord put in me was to tell the people that Christ has risen and that He is alive forevermore. The Lord called me to preach and teach the Good News of Jesus Christ the Messiah for He is the promised hope of salvation for anyone who believes and follows Him.

The Lord called me to go, not to worry about the how's. He provided for my family, and we didn't lack anything. Matthew 6:31-32 (GNT) says, "So do not start worrying: 'Where will my food come from? or my drink? or my clothes?' (These are the things the pagans are always concerned about.) Your Father in heaven knows that you need all these things."

I praise and glorify God for always being there!

By Alex Valenzuela

Chapter 25
Special Love For God's People

In 1994 when the Lord called me to go back to the jungles of Mexico, he gave me such a special love for the people there. Jeremiah 20:9 (GNT) says, "...then your message is like a fire burning deep within me..." God showers His pure love on us and doesn't want His people to be lost.

The Lord wanted me to share His love with the people in Mexico just as He shares His love with us. He wants to be part of their lives, to care for them. 1 Timothy 2:4-5 says, "who wants everyone to be saved and to come to know the truth. For there is one God, and there is one who brings God and human beings together, the man Christ Jesus."

When I first started breaking ground, many of these villages didn't have roads. It took anywhere from thirty minutes to two hours to walk to them. Many times I would witness late into the night, which means I often slept in the villages.

As I said earlier, this meant no electricity, no running water, and mosquitoes all over me.

The people didn't have much, and I didn't like sleeping in a one-room hut. So, I often slept outside wherever I felt comfortable. At times that meant I slept with the chickens. But I saw such a vast number of stars in the sky. Psalm 118:24 (NKJV) says, "This is the day the Lord has made; We will rejoice and be glad in it."

I previously mentioned that in the morning, the people would make me a fresh pot of coffee from the beans they had grown themselves. They also fed me black beans and eggs every day. One day I asked them to make beef soup for me, and I paid for all the ingredients. This beef soup was amazing. I thoroughly enjoyed it. So, they gave me some more the next day.

The third day they were ready to give me some more beef soup, but I asked them, "Where are you getting the money to buy all the ingredients?"

They said, "It is the same soup from three days ago."

They didn't have electricity, which meant no refrigeration. That explained why the food they served me sometimes had a smell to it. It also explains why I would have the runs for days after drinking a glass of orange juice or lemonade. I also learned that not everyone boiled the water. 1 Corinthians 10:27 (AMP) says, "If one of the unbelievers invites you [to a meal at his home] and you want to go, eat whatever is served to you without asking questions [about its source] for the sake of your conscience."

But I wouldn't have been there if God hadn't called me. Matthew 5:16 (NKJV) says, "Let your light so shine before men, that they may see your good works and glorify your Father in heaven."

When I first started working there, I had no credentials from a church organization. I met brother Dionicio from Mexico City about three months later. His organization was trying to start a mission but with no success. I invited him to our church service, and he joined us. He was surprised to see the villagers attending my services.

He asked me who I was affiliated with, and I told him I was a lone ranger in Mexico. He asked me if I would join his organization while working in Mexico, so my prayer was answered, and we worked well together. I needed them just as much as they needed me. So at that point, I had access to pastors and teachers. Ephesians 5:21 (KJV) says, "Submitting yourselves one to another in the fear of God."

Many times, the city authority tried to shut us down, but once they saw our credentials, they quit bothering us. When I was breaking ground somewhere else, brother Dionicio would attend to the missions, so I didn't need to rush back.

Out of fourteen missions, eleven became churches. As soon as a mission reached seventy-five members it went into church status, and we would bring in a pastor. The three that didn't become churches were farther away and therefore harder to reach. Teachers didn't like to travel on foot for two hours just to teach at a mission, and after a while, they would just quit.

After I returned home to the States, the Lord told me to

support brother Dionicio in the mission field. Brother Dionicio had a thriving business by Mexico City, and the Lord was telling him to let it go and take care of the missions. This was a hard decision for him because he had a family. So, I went back to the missions. As soon as I got off the bus, I ran into brother Dionicio, and he told me about the dreams God had given him. He asked me to visit one of the missions with him, and I agreed to go. We walked for two hours to visit the one that was the farthest away.

About halfway there, we stopped at a creek, and Dionicio was just standing in it, letting the flowing water cool his feet. He began to tell me what the Lord had told him, to move and live by the missions. As we talked, he showed me the calluses on his feet and said, "None of this bothers me because God has given me so much love for the people here."

At that moment I realized God had given him that same special love He had given me when I first started witnessing in those villages. I let him know that God had told me to support him and his wife. He said he was closing his business in Mexico City to live in the villages. Hebrews 13:16 (GNT) says, "Do not forget to do good and to help one another, because these are the sacrifices that please God."

Unfortunately, the people at one village he visited tied him to a tree. Thankfully, they released him the next day. 2 Timothy 1:7 (NKJV) says, "For God has not given us a spirit of fear, but of power and of love and of a sound mind."

We prayed for days over this village. Then we went back to the same area, witnessed to them, and God broke the hardness of the people's hearts. Ezekiel 11:19 (ESV) says, "And I will give them one heart, and a new spirit I will put within them. I will remove the heart of stone from their flesh and give them a heart of flesh."

My life was threatened many times in that area. They would wave machetes at me and tell me, "You will die if you go." But God told me that He had my back. Acts 18:19-10 (NKJV) says, "Do not be afraid, but speak, and do not keep silent; for I am with you, and no one will attack you to hurt you; for I have many people in this city."

About 6 o'clock one morning, the villagers saw me and got on their knees and started praising God. I asked the interpreter what was going on, and he told me the people were happy to see me alive because of those who were waiting to ambush me and kill me the previous night. God was protecting me and I didn't even know it.

That same day a lady who couldn't walk asked me to pray for her. After I did so, God healed her completely. As it turned out, she was related to one of the people who were going to ambush me. Psalm 36:7 (GNT) says, "How precious, O God, is your constant love! We find protection under the shadow of your wings."

Believe me when I say that many nights I would cry to God and say, "Why me?" God protected me there because nobody ever laid a hand on me. Joshua 1:9 (GNT) says, "Remember that I have commanded you to be determined and confident! Do not be afraid or discouraged, for I, the Lord your God, am with you wherever you go."

I praise and glorify the Lord for He is merciful!

Chapter 26
Giving Your Best

Acts 20:35 (AMP) says, "In everything I showed you by example that by working hard in this way you must help the weak and remember the words of the Lord Jesus, that He Himself said, It is more blessed and brings greater joy to give than to receive."

Has God ever told you to give your best? Having agape love in your life isn't a matter of emotions but a matter of willingness to do things that benefit the needs of others. I had two cars, one old and one fairly new car that I had just finished paying off. My wife and I had been married only two years, and we had one child, so we weren't yet financially stable. So I felt as though we had accomplished something big when we paid off the loan on the car.

But after the loan was paid off, God said to me, "Give your car to the pastor in Progresso, Mexico." This is the same pastor who was my translator in the jungle of Hildago. I had decided to give my older car away, but the Lord said to me, "Give your best."

We set a date to take the car into Mexico. Not only were we giving our car away, but we had to deliver it. I wasn't a happy camper, but I was being obedient to God's instructions. 1 Chronicles 29:14 (NLT) says, "But who am I, and who are my people, that we could give anything to you? Everything we have has come from you, and we give you only what you first gave us!"

I let the church know what God had said to me and told them when we would deliver the car. The day we headed out, I went by the pastor's house so he could pray for our trip, but he tried to talk me out of it. He said, "Are you sure it is God telling you to do this and not your emotions?"

I told my pastor, "God is telling me to give my best, and He will provide for this trip."

We had only a hundred dollars in our account, and we had to take two cars to Mexico, one to give to the church and the other to drive home in. Plus the drive took about twelve hours, and we had to buy gas and food along the way.

When we were about six hours into the trip, my old car broke down, but we were near a rest stop. The little lying devil was at it again, trying to prevent me from giving my best. We were one hour from San Antonio, Texas. My family and I drove the rest of the way and stayed with a friend.

The following day I went to see my friend, Jose, and when he saw me, he just smiled and hugged me. I told him my car had broken down, and I needed it fixed. He took the day off and said, "Let us go find a dolly and pick up your car. I want to be a blessing to you, so I'm not going to charge you a cent to fix it. Just pay for the parts."

I had a Bible study that night. When it was over and everyone was leaving, someone shook my hand and put money in it. I prayed the Lord would put a special blessing on him and his family, and it was enough to pay for all the parts.

The next day, Jose was fixing the car, and another friend came by and said, "Feed your worker" and put money in my shirt pocket. My wife bought food for everyone there.

The car was fixed, and we were on our way again. While we were driving, the Lord spoke to me and said, "Go to Paul's house."

I said, "Lord, Paul is never home; he is a busy man."

But the Lord said, "Go."

So, I turned the car in the direction of Paul's home. Once I arrived, I knocked on his door and Paul answered. I was shocked to see him, but he just smiled and said, "What are you doing here?"

I said, "I am giving a car away in Mexico. As I was driving, the Lord said to me, 'Go see Paul,' so here I am."

We visited for a while, and he told me how God had truly blessed him. He went into the kitchen and called me and said, "The Lord just spoke to me in my spirit and told me that you are broke and to give you money."

I broke down and cried because Paul was the first-person God had shown that it was His will for him to give me money. From the beginning of the trip, I had been fasting because I had to trust in God to deliver the car. Ezra 8:23 (GNT) says, "So we fasted and prayed for God to protect us, and he answered our prayers."

I never told anyone or gave any indication that we were broke. So, only God could have shown Paul that we needed money.

Paul gave us a check for a large sum. So, I cashed the check and headed to Mexico.

When we arrived at the pastor's house, the Lord said to me, "Give half the money away." But because of all my struggles we'd had on this trip, I decided to give only 25 percent of it.

The next day we were heading toward the border and the Lord said to me, "Did I not tell you to give half?" So, I turned the car around, went back to the pastor's house, and gave him the rest of the money.

He broke down and cried. He said, "We were robbed, and we didn't want to tell you because you were giving us a car." I felt so ashamed and wished that God had revealed the situation to me. This experience taught me that when God is telling me to do something, I need to just do it and not overthink it.

When we arrived home, we went to church and testified how God had blessed our trip. God wanted to bless the church I attended, but they refused to believe God was telling us to give our car away. They were looking at me as though I ran with my emotions. They never believed God would tell someone to give their best when they have nothing. So, God gave the blessing to others who were willing to listen to Him even though they didn't know the situation.

Within a short period of time, the Lord blessed us with a brand-new van paid for in full.

To this day, the Lord has always blessed us with new cars, and they are always paid in full.

To God be all the Glory!

Chapter 27
"Witchcraft"
The Necklace Charm

Ephesians 6:16 (GNT) says, "At all times carry faith as a shield; for with it you will be able to put out all the burning arrows shot by the Evil One."

How do you gain faith as a shield in your life? By putting a considerable amount of time in with the Lord, reading and meditating on His Word, praying, fasting, and testifying about what the Lord has done.

In football, there are many different positions. The players have to prepare for every game by watching and studying the films of previous games to understand their opponents. The quarterback's job, for example, is to learn the other team's defense. Once he knows how the other teams are going to defend against his offense, he knows how to attack.

Every player on every team has to train to become faster, stronger, and wiser. This means maintaining a certain diet and training four to eight hours a day, not five, ten, or fifteen minutes.

The Christian player has to study his opponent to know how to attack and defend against him. We do this by studying the Word of God and maintaining a certain diet of fasting, praying, meditating, and testifying. The closer we get to the Lord, the more we will carry the shield of faith to put out all the flaming arrows the little lying devil throws at us.

When we are rooted in the Word of God, we are not fazed when trouble comes our way. We know in whom we trust. James 4:7 (AMP) says, "So submit to [the authority of] God. Resist the devil [stand firm against him] and he will flee from you."

We already have the victory over Satan's schemes. We just have to know who we are in Christ. 2 Corinthians 2:11 (The Voice) says, "It's my duty to make sure that Satan does not win even a small victory over us, for we don't want to be naïve and then fall prey to his schemes."

In 1995, when I was working in Hidalgo, a young man had traveled to Mexico City and bought a necklace, which he constantly wore around his neck and held it as though it was something special. Upon his return home, he became sick. I was asked to pray for him, and I said, "Let's go."

When I saw him, he looked as though something was sucking the life out of him and that he was about to die. The Lord showed me it was the fruit of the spirit of divination. I asked him how long he'd had the necklace he was always wearing, and he told me where and when he bought it. I explained to him that he was wearing an amulet that someone had cast a spell on and that he would be sick as long as he wore it. Merriam-Webster defines an amulet as a "charm (such as an ornament) often inscribed with a magic incantation or symbol to aid the wearer or protect against evil (such as disease or witchcraft)."

He did not believe what I was saying to him and did not let me pray for him. I told him I would be back in a few days to visit him. When I returned, I discovered he had become even sicker, so I asked again if he wanted me to pray for him. He said, "Yes, please pray for me."

I said, "Give me the necklace so I can destroy it."

He said, "But I paid a lot of money for it." He had spent all the money he had on that necklace, so losing it was going to be a real blow for him.

I decided to buy it from him, and when he handed it to me, I cursed the spirit of divination to its root and threw the necklace into the fire.

The following day I visited the young man, and I saw that he was completely healed and full of life again. Deuteronomy 18:10-11 (GNT) says, "Don't sacrifice your children in the fires on your altars; and don't let your people practice divination or look for omens or use spells or charms, and don't let them consult the spirits of the dead." The young man introduced me to his family and friends, who heard the Word of God, and many were saved.

The devil tries to make us think that his wiles are effective. He hits us during a crisis and tries to make us think we have never been healed. But the Lord will fight side by side with us to defeat the devil's schemes. We just need to put on the full armor of God, trust His power, and draw strength from Him. Ephesians 6:10-13 (ESV) says:

"Finally, be strong in the Lord and in the strength of his might. Put on the whole armor of God, that you may be able to stand against the schemes of the devil. For we do not wrestle against flesh and blood, but against the rulers, against the authorities, against the cosmic powers over this present darkness, against the spiritual forces of evil in the heavenly places. Therefore take up the whole armor of God, that you may be able to withstand in the evil day, and having done all, to stand firm."

"Yet in all these things we are more than conquerors through Him who loved us" (Romans 8:37 NKJV). God's Word is a powerful weapon when we stand firm on it. In the same way, prayer is essential to combating the enemy.

To God be all the Glory!

Chapter 28
Spiritual Weapons In Mexico

Joshua 1:9 (GNT) says, "Remember that I have commanded you to be determined and confident! Do not be afraid or discouraged, for I, the Lord your God, am with you wherever you go."

Have bad things ever come your way after you have done something good? In 1995, we bought a broken-down Grand Marquis and fixed it. The Lord had blessed us with some money, and we wanted to put it toward the kingdom of God. So we bought three hundred Bibles to give to people who had just gotten saved so each could have his or her own personal Bible, and twenty more expensive Bibles to give to teachers.

I set a date for when I was going to Hildago. As always, my pastor and I prayed for my trip before I took off. About two hours after I left, my car broke down on a country road. Praise God, I wasn't far from a small store that had a phone booth. I called my friends, Michael and Matt, and told them I had broken down in the middle of nowhere, and I asked them to bring a trailer.

Jeremiah 29:11-12 (GNT) says, "I alone know the plans I have for you, plans to bring you prosperity and not disaster, plans to bring about the future you hope for. Then you will call to me. You will come and pray to me, and I will answer you."

They hooked the trailer to their truck and then picked me up, no questions asked. As it turned out, I needed a new transmission.

I went back home, found a used transmission, and replaced it. Three days later I was off to Mexico. It would take twelve hours to get to Reynosa, and from there another fourteen to reach my destination. I was back on the road, taking the same route as I did before.

When I am all alone, I do silly things like a child does when he is going on a family vacation, like putting my hand out the window and playing with the air. I also like putting my head out the window just to enjoy the rushing air. Just like that commercial of the dog sitting in the back of the car, with his head out the window, enjoying the rushing air. Plus, driving alone gives me time to talk, praise, cry, worship, and meditate on God.

On this day I was having a good ol' time with God, and all of a sudden buzzards started coming out of nowhere and were landing on a fence post on the right side of the road. They had their wings spread as they were landing. Even after they had landed, all of them stayed in the same position, with their wings spread.

For the next two miles, I saw nothing but buzzards on the fence post with their wings spread. It was as if the king was passing by, and everyone was kneeling to give reverence. I really believe the buzzards were spreading their wings to worship God as He passed by because He was in the car with me. I have traveled this road for years, but I haven't seen the buzzards since that day.

Here is a picture of three buzzards on a fencepost, so you can get an idea of what I saw. Just imagine a buzzard on every fence post giving reverence with their wings spread for two miles. Praise God!

At the border, I got the proper documentation to travel farther into Mexico. When I arrived at the next checkpoint about twenty miles outside Reynosa, the officer asked me, "What do you have in your car?"

I said, "Bibles."

He said, "Push the button," which I did, and it was red. That means my car was going to be searched. He said, "Open the trunk of your car," so I did. He saw lots of Bibles and said, "You are smuggling illegal weapons into Mexico." He handcuffed me as if I were a criminal and took me inside the building.

The captain of the guard approached me and said they were going to lock me up. He said, "I need you to tell me exactly what you said before you pushed that button." While the captain was talking to me, Isaiah 41:13 (GNT) came to mind: "I am the Lord your God; I strengthen you and tell you, 'Do not be afraid; I will help you.'"

I said, "The officer asked me what I had in the car, and I told him, 'Bibles.' Then he said, 'Push the button, so I did, and it was red. So, he searched my car.'"

He smiled, shook his head in disbelief, and said, "You had Bibles. Those aren't physical weapons." The more he thought about the incident, the more he chuckled, and then he said, "I'm a Christian."

At that moment I knew God was going to get me out of this mess. The captain of the guard explained to me that the officer at the checkpoint was trying to bring charges against me for trying to smuggle illegal weapons into Mexico. As he was chuckling and nodding his head, he said, "I guess the Bibles are weapons, but they are spiritual weapons."

2 Corinthians 10:4 (GNT) says, "The weapons we use in our fight are not the world's weapons but God's powerful weapons, which we use to destroy strongholds…" After investigating the incident thoroughly, the captain released me from custody. He said, "You cannot take those spiritual weapons any farther into Mexico," and told me I had to return to the United States.

As I was driving toward Reynosa, a lot of thoughts were running through my head. Psalm 94:18-19 (AMP) says, "If I say, 'My foot has slipped,' Your compassion and lovingkindness, O Lord, will hold me up. When my anxious thoughts multiply within me, Your comforts delight me."

I said to myself, "That little lying devil is trying to prevent me from giving these Bibles away." So I decided to go see the pastor in Progresso. I went to his home and told him about my little adventure. He laughed so hard, nodding his head in disbelief, the same way the captain of the guard did. We were both laughing, having a good time in the Lord. He said, "I have been praying to the Lord for help in getting Bibles because we have had so many new converts. I want them to have their own Bibles, but I don't have the money to buy them.

I said to him, "Those Bibles are staying in Mexico," and I gave him all the Bibles I had. Romans 8:28 (GNT) says, "We know that in all things God works for good with those who love him, those whom he has called according to his purpose." To God be all the glory.

As I was crossing the border back into the United States, the agent for the border patrol asked me why I went to Mexico, and I replied, "to give Bibles away."

The officer looked angry and said, "Pull your car into that station," where the border patrol fully inspected my poor car. That little lying devil was trying to pay me back for giving the Bibles away. I knew they couldn't arrest me for smuggling illegal weapons since there were no Bibles in the car. After a long search, they released my car, and I was on my way home.

I was driving home, praising the Lord, and enjoying myself. When I was an hour out of McAllen, Texas, a state trooper saw me, made a U-turn, and drove behind me for a long while. Next thing I knew three state troopers were following me and they pulled me over. *Now what?* I thought.

One was in front of me, one was behind me, and one was on the side of me. One of them said, "You are being detained while they get a warrant to search your car." I guess that little lying devil was still angry.

While we were waiting, I asked the state troopers why they thought I was doing something illegal. Their response was "The year and make of your car. Most drug smugglers use this year to make and transport drugs."

"That's ridiculous," I told them. "You don't need a search warrant. I give you permission. The faster you search my car, the faster I can get home."

After they searched my car, one of the troopers gave me some advice. He said, "Consider selling your car."

When I got home, I gave the car away so I would never have that problem again. 2 Corinthians 9:12 (AMP) says, "For the ministry of this service offering is not only supplying the needs of the saints God's people, but is also overflowing through many expressions of thanksgiving to God."

The Lord blessed us with some more money, and I went back into the mission field. Brother Dionicio and I went into Mexico City, bought the Bibles, and gave them to the new converts. That little lying devil wasn't going to stop us from being a blessing to God's people.

I praise and glorify my Lord and Savior of my soul!

Chapter 29
"Witchcraft" and Paralyzed Woman Healed

While traveling through the jungles of Mexico, I saw many incidents involving magic, omens, sorcerers, witchcraft, and enchantment. On the cross, Christ disarmed the rulers, authorities, and supernatural forces of evil that operate against us. 1 Peter 3:21-22 (ASV) says all authority has been given to Him "...through the resurrection of Jesus Christ; who is on the right hand of God, having gone into heaven; angels and authorities and powers being made subject unto him."

Look at what the scriptures say about magic, omens, sorcerers, witchcraft, and enchantment. In Exodus 7:11 (AMP) "Then Pharaoh called for the wise men [skilled in magic and omens] and the sorcerers [skilled in witchcraft], and they also, these magicians (soothsayer-priests) of Egypt, did the same with their secret arts and enchantments." Exodus 7:22

(AMP) says, "But the magicians of Egypt did the same by their secret arts and enchantments; so Pharaoh's heart was hardened."

One day I was asked to pray for a lady who was completely paralyzed from her neck down. I always asked God for direction before I went to any new ground. I usually did this by fasting for a couple of days. This time I fasted for five days because I didn't know what was there. It was an hour away from where I was staying, and I wanted God's approval to go.

Once God gave me the okay, I visited the young lady and asked her how she became paralyzed. She said her husband saw her talking to a stranger, who was asking her for directions. When she got home, her husband beat her with the heel of her shoe, tore the middle of her back, and left her paralyzed.

The people there with me turned her over so I could see the wound. It had puss and blood on it as if it were a new wound. I asked how long she had been like this. They said, "Six months."

She had been taken to the doctor, who, after many tests, told her that her nerves were dead and that she would be paralyzed for life. I asked her if she believed God could heal her. She just smiled and said, "I hope so." I taught her the Word of God and told her the God I serve loved her and would heal her.

After praying for her, I grabbed her arm and pulled her forward, and she just fell back onto her bed. So, I commanded healing to go into her whole body in Jesus' name, and I pulled her forward again. Again, her body fell back onto the bed. I grabbed her a third time, and said, "You are healed in Jesus' name," and pulled her forward again.

This time, as she was falling back, her body strengthened, and she caught herself. She started moving her arms and twisting her body from side to side. Her legs started shaking so hard she started crying. She said, "I can feel my legs."

I asked her, "Do you believe God can heal you?"

She smiled and said, "Jesus just did."

God did a miracle and I praise Him for that. On my way back down the mountain I was pondering the book of Acts where Simon (Peter) went to Lydda, and prayed for someone who was paralyzed. Acts 9:33-35 (GNT) says:

"There he met a man named Aeneas, who was paralyzed and had not been able to get out of bed for eight years. 'Aeneas,' Peter said to him, 'Jesus Christ makes you well. Get up and make your bed.' At once Aeneas got up. All the people living in Lydda and Sharon saw him, and they turned to the Lord."

After God performed this miracle, the people of that village started turning to the Lord.

About 11 o'clock that night, brother Santos came to me and said, "We need to go back to the lady you prayed for this morning. She is dying."

We took off with flashlights, up the mountain and back to the lady's house. When we arrived, I saw the veins on the side of her head thumping. 2 Corinthians 2:11 (The Voice) says, "It's my duty to make sure that Satan does not win even a small victory over us, for we don't want to be naïve and then fall prey to his schemes."

I told brother Santos, "It is witchcraft." I put my hands on her and cursed the spirit of divination to the root in the name of Jesus. Immediately she was calm and healed, and the veins in her head returned to normal. 2 Corinthians 10:4 (GNT) says, "The weapons we use in our fight are not the world's weapons but God's powerful weapons, which we use to destroy strongholds."

About 12:30 a.m. I found myself frustrated with what I was seeing, so I decided to teach against witchcraft. The first scripture I used was Deuteronomy 18:10-11 (GNT) "Don't sacrifice your children in the fires on your altars; and don't let your people practice divination or look for omens or use spells or charms, and don't let them consult the spirits of the dead."

The young lady's mother and father were witch doctors, and they had invoked an evil spirit on their daughter. So, I told them, "There are consequences when you practice witchcraft and this is a good example. The magic spell you intended for someone else just bounced back to your daughter. You could have killed her." Leviticus 19:31 (AMP) says, "Do not turn to mediums [who pretend to consult the dead] or to spiritists [who have spirits of divination]; do not seek them out to be defiled by them. I am the Lord your God."

That night they repented and gave their lives to God. The next day I went back to check on the family, and the young lady's parents told me to follow them. They took me to a large, empty room. I didn't understand what they were doing or why I was there. At first I thought, *Do they want me to stay here with them?*

They said, "This is the room where we used to practice witchcraft, but now we have cleared it out. We will never do those things again. Now we have Christ in our lives."

I checked on the young lady, and she was so happy. She showed me her back where the wound was. It had completely scabbed over. Only God can do these kinds of miracles. There is power and authority in the name of Christ.

I praise and glorify the Lord!

Chapter 30
"Witchcraft"
San Luis Potosí, Mexico

Genesis 4:6-7 (AMP) says, "And the Lord said to Cain, "Why are you so angry? And why do you look annoyed? If you do well [believing Me and doing what is acceptable and pleasing to Me], will you not be accepted? And if you do not do well [but ignore My instruction], sin crouches at your door; its desire is for you [to overpower you], but you must master it."

Satan is looking for an open door in our lives to get in. An open door will let sin in, which can, in turn, control our lives. We cannot leave any such foothold for the devil. He is working hard to undermine what God is doing in us. He exists, but we don't have to live in fear of the supernatural. God has given us a powerful weapon against temptation and accusation: His Word.

I attended a church that supported missions in San Luis Potosi, Mexico. One day the pastor called me to his office and asked if I would be willing to observe the missions there.

The missionary the church supported was brother Daniel, who had three missions there. I agreed to go for six weeks.

When we first arrived, I felt an evil presence in the air. I told brother Daniel that I was going to lock myself up for a week to pray and fast. I wanted God to show me what I was going to be fighting in the spiritual world.

Brother Daniel was bothered by what I said because he couldn't believe there was anything evil in the air. I didn't have time to try to explain what I was feeling, so I went to the room and closed the door.

After a week of fasting, the Lord showed me the spirit of divination had a strong hold there even though brother Daniel said he had never had a problem with any demonic force there. Ephesians 6:12 (NLT) says, "For we are not fighting against flesh-and-blood enemies, but against evil rulers and authorities of the unseen world, against mighty powers in this dark world, and against evil spirits in the heavenly places."

We started visiting people that day, and we invited them to the service that night, where I taught the people how to break the strongholds of the little lying devil and defeat him. Ephesians 6:10-11 (TLB) says, "Last of all I want to remind you that your strength must come from the Lord's mighty power within you. Put on all of God's armor so that you will be able to stand safe against all strategies and tricks of Satan."

Most people don't realize the spirit of divination is the evil root, and its fruits are witchcraft, magic, enchantment, and spell casting, among other things. I started teaching the people how Jesus Christ had stripped the devil of all his powers. Colossians 2:15 (AMP) says, "When He had disarmed the rulers and authorities [those supernatural forces of evil operating against us], He made a public example of them [exhibiting them as captives in His triumphal procession], having triumphed over them through the cross."

That night I prayed for the people who were sick, and God healed those in the service who needed healing. I also cursed the root of the spirit of divination and it died. Once the root died, the fruit also died. Now that the root and the fruit were dead, the curse was dissolved and the sickness was gone.

For the next three nights in the services, God continued to heal the people who were sick. Ephesians 6:16 (CEB) says, "Above all, carry the shield of faith so that you can extinguish the flaming arrows of the evil one."

On the third night, I fell asleep. At about 2 a.m. I awakened gasping for air. An invisible hand had me by the throat, and I couldn't breathe. So I rebuked the evil spirit in my mind, but it couldn't hear my thoughts.

God intervened, and it released me. Then I saw a vision of fifteen or more witches around a campfire, coming against me. But 2 Thessalonians 3:3 (CEB) says, "But the Lord is faithful and will give you strength and protect you from the evil one."

I was so angry (and I believe it was Godly anger), so I started teaching the people about the power of God. I taught them how to disarm and destroy the strongholds with the Word of God. 2 Corinthians 10:4-5 (ERV) says, "The weapons we use are not human ones. Our weapons have power from God and can destroy the enemy's strong places."

When I was in the military, I noticed there were lots of soldiers but few warriors. The Roman General Hericletus once said, "Of every one hundred men [they send me], ten shouldn't even be there, eighty are nothing but targets, nine are real fighters... We are lucky to have them... They make the battle. Ah, but the one, one of them is a Warrior... and he will bring the others back."

I had a whole month to build Godly warriors, not soldiers, and I was committed to doing so. I started having classes, teaching the Word of God all day long. No disrespect toward brother Daniel, who didn't believe in the demonic force that was there, but the church members understood something evil was there, and they were determined to learn the Word to defeat it.

I kept teaching that Christ has risen, that He is alive in us, and that we have authority. Luke 10:19 (AMP) says, "Listen carefully: I have given you authority [that you now possess] to tread on serpents and scorpions, and [the ability to exercise authority] over all the power of the enemy (Satan); and nothing will [in any way] harm you."

And Colossians 2:9-10 (CEB) says, "For in Him all the fullness of Deity (the Godhead) dwells in bodily form [completely expressing the divine essence of God]. And in Him you have been made complete [achieving spiritual stature through Christ], and He is the head over all rule and authority [of every angelic and earthly power]."

They had been freed from the satanic power that had a hold on them. They were making sure to learn the Word of God so that they didn't go back into captivity.

I had a German Shepherd that I had trained. She always knew when I was going to give a command. I would tell her to sit or lie down, and she would stay in the position I commanded until I gave her another command. No matter which command I gave her, she obeyed.

One day she chewed my water hose, and I called her to let her know. She knew I was angry with her just by the tone of my voice. I would point my finger and say, "Get! I don't want to see you," and she would run and hide. I had authority over my dog.

We have that same power and authority over Satan and his followers. We just have to command them as we would command a dog. When we speak our commands, we have to speak to them with authority. Satan tries to make us think he still has power, but he can only toil with our minds. Jesus Christ has stripped him of all his power and nailed it to the cross. In all these things we are victorious because Christ lives in us.

Divination opens a door into the spiritual world, an outlet for the enemy. According to the Merriam-Webster dictionary, divination means, "the art or practice that seeks to foresee or foretell future events or discover hidden knowledge usually by the interpretation of omens or by the aid of supernatural powers."

The Word of God tells us to stay away from this kind of stuff because it blinds our minds. Deuteronomy 18:10-12 (AMP) says:

There shall not be found among you anyone who makes his son or daughter pass through the fire [as a sacrifice], one who uses divination and fortune-telling, one who practices witchcraft, or one who interprets omens, or a sorcerer, or one who casts a charm or spell, or a medium, or a spiritist, or a necromancer [who seeks the dead]. For everyone who does these things is utterly repulsive to the Lord; and because of these detestable practices the Lord your God is driving them out before you.

After observing the situation there, I determined they needed pastors to take over the missions. Each mission had more than seventy-five members. We always have the victory over Satan's schemes; we just have to know who we are in Christ. Ephesians 6:10-11 (CEV) says, "Finally, let the mighty strength of the Lord make you strong. Put on all the armor that God gives, so you can defend yourself against the devil's tricks."

I praise and glorify the Lord for always watching over me!

Chapter 31
"Witchcraft"
Spirit of Divination

Genesis 4:6-7 (AMP) says, "And the Lord said to Cain, "Why are you so angry? And why do you look annoyed? If you do well [believing Me and doing what is acceptable and pleasing to Me], will you not be accepted? And if you do not do well [but ignore My instruction], sin crouches at your door; its desire is for you [to overpower you], but you must master it."

And Romans 8:5-8 (NLT) says:

> Those who are dominated by the sinful nature think about sinful things, but those who are controlled by the Holy Spirit think about things that please the Spirit. So letting your sinful nature control your mind leads to death. But letting the Spirit control your mind leads to life and peace. For the sinful nature is always hostile to God. It never did

obey God's laws, and it never will. That's why those who are still under the control of their sinful nature can never please God.

I was visiting my brother, Hector, when he received a phone call. When he hung up the phone, he asked me if I would accompany him to the hospital. They asked him if we could pray for a lady who was dying of cancer. The doctors didn't give her long to live.

We went to the hospital, and when I saw her, I saw it was the spirit of divination. We prayed against that spirit and God healed her instantly. Merriam-Webster says divination is "the art or practice that seeks to foresee or foretell future events or discover hidden knowledge usually by the interpretation of omens or by the aid of supernatural powers." The doctors couldn't find anything wrong with her, but they kept her overnight just to observe her. She died that night.

The next day her family told us she had died because her throat had swelled up. The cancer was gone, so the devil used other means to kill her.

I went to my room and cried bitterly unto the Lord. I said to Him, "You healed her. Why did you let her die?" It felt as though everything was a lie, and I wanted to quit ministering to people.

After a few hours of crying unto the Lord, He said to me, "How can she defend herself if she doesn't know my Word?"

I said, "But she is a Christian and she has been in church all her life."

At that moment Hosea 4:6 (AMP) came to mind: "My people are destroyed for lack of knowledge [of My law, where I reveal My will]." I realized at that moment that most people don't know how to use the Word of God to fight, because they have never been taught.

Many don't understand the enemy at hand. Ephesians 6:13 (GNT) says, "So put on God's armor now! Then when the evil day comes, you will be able to resist the enemy's attacks; and after fighting to the end, you will still hold your ground."

From that day on I would teach people how to defend themselves using the Word of God before I prayed for them.

To God be all the Glory!

As I have traveled through churches, I have noticed that most Christians say, "I am saved, and the devil cannot touch me." That's a true statement if you're living a righteous life with God. But what about those in the church who don't live righteous lives and instead fulfill the desires of the flesh? Some are letting anger control their lives. Others can't forgive something from the past. Ephesians 4:27 (NLT) says, "for anger gives a foothold to the devil."

After I bought a house, I noticed that both sides of our street were full of cars. I wondered if any of those people worked. If they did, then why were all the cars parked there? One day I was in prayer at about two or three in the morning, and something that smelled like sulfur came into the house. Immediately I started rebuking the spirit of divination and asked God to show me where it was coming from. The Lord showed me that it was coming from a house where a woman who specialized in palm reading lived, three houses down.

Now that I had a clear understanding of my enemy and what she did, I knew how to pray. So, that night I started praying for her salvation, and the Lord said, "Go and stand in front of her house and pray."

I did this every night until her daughter knocked on my door and said, "My mother sent me here to see if she can talk to you."

I responded, "Who is your mother?"

And she said, "We live three houses down."

I went with the young girl to meet her mother, who said, "Why do you come to my house every night and pray? I see you every single night standing on the sidewalk in front of my house, and you are praying with your hands up in the air at two in the morning."

I explained that the Lord had sent me to pray for her salvation, and she said, "I am saved, and I go to church."

I found it pretty frightening that she was going to church and calling herself a Christian, and the rest of the church members didn't have a clue. What really got me was that she was saying the devil couldn't touch her because she was saved, thinking palm reading wasn't of the devil. All those who use divination are partnering with the devil to work against the kingdom of God and His righteousness on earth.

Jeremiah 14:14 says, "And the Lord said to me: 'The prophets are prophesying lies in my name. I did not send them, nor did I command them or speak to them. They are prophesying to you a lying vision, worthless divination, and the deceit of their own minds.'"

I said to her, "You might be going to church, but you are not saved." You need to repent and accept Jesus as your personal Savior and follow His ways.

To God be all the Glory!

One day, when I lived in San Antonio, I was in church and a beautiful lady, full of bruises, came in. I had never seen her before, and I asked some of the church members if she was in an abusive marriage. They said she was married to an unbeliever, and he abused her.

Her husband was paying a witch doctor to cast a spell on her so he could dominate her. So, at church I prayed against the spirit of divination he had cast on her. 2 Corinthians 2:11 (The Voice) says, "It's my duty to make sure that Satan does not win even a small victory over us, for we don't want to be naïve and then fall prey to his schemes."

At once God broke the spell. She said, "I don't know why I allowed him to do what he wants with me. It is as if he has full control over me." The blinders had been removed from her eyes, and she was seeing clearly.

Her life seemed to be better for about three weeks, and then she showed up to church again full of bruises. Her husband would beat her, and she would say, "I love him deeply. He didn't mean to hit me."

So I prayed for her again, and once again God broke the spell. She asked me why this was happening to her since she was saved. I told her that sometimes we leave a door open to the enemy without realizing it. Then I told her I was going to teach her how to defend herself against the wiles of the devil using the Word of God.

Once she started learning how to pray against the spirit of divination, her life changed for the better. Ephesians 6:10-11 (CEV) says, "Finally, let the mighty strength of the Lord make you strong. Put on all the armor that God gives, so you can defend yourself against the devil's tricks." By this point, he was having a hard time dominating her with magic. She started having a closer relationship with the Lord and she was living a righteous life.

It is sad to say, but I have seen this with so many church members. If I try to tell them what they're facing, they fight me tooth and nail and say, "It's not true. I'm saved and they can't touch me." Now the works of the flesh are plain. Read Galatians 5:19-21. Remember that "sin crouches at your door; its desire is for you [to overpower you], but you must master it" (Genesis 4:7, AMP).

To God be all the Glory!

By Alex Valenzuela

Chapter 32
Equipping God's People

Ephesians 4:11-13 (NLT) says:

Now these are the gifts Christ gave to the church: the apostles, the prophets, the evangelists, and the pastors and teachers. Their responsibility is to equip God's people to do his work and build up the church, the body of Christ. This will continue until we all come to such unity in our faith and knowledge of God's Son that we will be mature in the Lord, measuring up to the full and complete standard of Christ.

In 2000, my overseer called me to do a work for a troubled church that had started constructing the church building, but the city inspector stopped the construction because they were trying to build it without having a permit. They had bought the materials and five acres of land, but the materials were just lying on the ground. The concrete for the foundation had been finished, and a water well was in place. But the congregation had formed another church elsewhere. My job was to finish the project and sell it.

When I arrived, I discovered there were no church funds to finish the project. So, I had a long talk with the overseer, and we came up with a solution. We took a picture of the foundation and the building materials on the ground. The overseer spoke with pastors of large congregations in different states to see who would sponsor sections of the project. Our priority was to erect the building, and we had a church reach out and sponsor us. We took pictures of all phases of the project like plumbing, electrical, walls, ceiling, and once we finished, we took a final picture and sent it to the church that sponsored that section, showing it had been completed.

While I was waiting for money to come in, I would visit people I had met. Once the shell had been completed, the people I visited started coming to church. When we reached thirty members, I knew I had some teachers and future pastors, so I started training and equipping God's people to do His work.

We had them teach or preach on Wednesday and Sunday nights, and before long we reached seventy-five members. One day I spoke with a man who visited our church and discovered he was witnessing at the local jails. We visited for hours, and I started asking him questions to find out more about him. He reminded me so much of myself when I was in the prison ministry.

I understood what he needed, so I put him in charge of the jail ministry we formed that day and gave him his credentials to present to the jail, showing them the church was backing him in the ministry. Every time he would visit the jailhouse, he would testify what God was doing in this ministry.

Next we started passing out food boxes to the poor. Every two months, we gave out 900 pounds of beans. We put beans, rice, potatoes, and cornmeal into every food box. My wife started a women's ministry that met once a week. We also had a potluck that became a monthly tradition.

To get the children involved in God's work, I put coins into a five-gallon water jug. I would shake it during every service and tell the children to bring their coins to give an offering. I picked up the jug after every service. The children loved being part of the ministry.

The older members would call the children to them and give them coins so that the church could keep seeing the excitement. During the testimony service, many of the children would testify what God was doing in their lives or sing a song for the Lord.

So, now we had teachers, preachers, a prison ministry, and givers in the church. I started seeing the church maturing in the Lord. They started having the fullness of Christ. Many times the presence of the Lord was so strong after the praise and worship service. Then we would form a circle and invite anyone who needed healing or a blessing from God to walk into the middle of the circle.

In one accord we would pray, and the Lord would move in a unique way. One day we formed a circle and a church member asked if we could pray for his brother, who lived in

Denver and had cirrhosis of the liver. We all prayed, and we felt the presence of the Lord.

About a week later, the church member stepped up to the mic and testified that his brother had a new liver. Praise be to God.

One Sunday night, one of the church members brought into the service a man who had open sores all over his body. They were two to three inches in diameter, and he'd had them for years. It looked as though he had leprosy. He said the doctors had tried everything but with no success. So, we formed a circle and put him in the middle, and with one accord we prayed for him.

About four days later, the brother who had brought him to the service took me to see him. When he saw us, he came running to us, showing us his sores. He said, "Look at my sores; they have scabs on them." He was completely healed. To God be all the glory.

By this time, the church members were no longer spiritual babies. They were maturing in the Lord. They started bringing sick people to our church so we could pray for them. They weren't chasing the ministry of healing because we had it in our church. They weren't being tossed by the wind with doubts and fear. They were growing in love and becoming more and more like Christ.

The future laborers were there. We just needed to recognize what was in the midst of the church. 1 Corinthians 12:27 (NIV) says, "Now you are the body of Christ, and each one of you is a part of it."

And 1 Corinthians 6:17 (AMP) says, "But the one who is united and joined to the Lord is one spirit with Him."

Obviously then, we didn't sell the building. We kept it in place with a new pastor. This story also happened to all the missions we started in Mexico.

The Church is the body of Christ. That is me! It is you! He needs you to go and witness and win souls. "Go!"

I praise and glorify the Lord!

Chapter 33
Joy in the Midst of Tragedy

Psalm 51:12 (ASV) says, "Restore unto me the joy of thy salvation...."

And Psalm 16:11 (ASV) says, "...In thy presence is fulness of joy...."

Have you ever cried out "Why me?" to God? Have you ever wondered why bad things happen to righteous people? Over the years I have seen so many people suffering, and they don't have the strength to fight any longer. Many times they feel that living is pointless, especially when they don't know why tragedy has fallen upon them.

When I see how people in the Bible trusted God to help them regardless of their situations, I see the mindset of the believer who doesn't know God is in his or her midst.

Job endured tremendous hardships, but he didn't know why. In Job 1, God is bragging to Satan that Job is a perfect and upright man. Satan, that little lying devil, tells God, "Take your protection off him, and we will see what he does."

Job was indeed a righteous man, and he had a good life for a long time. God had truly blessed him and had a hedge of protection around him and his belongings. Job 1:10 (CEV) says, "You are like a wall protecting not only him, but his entire family and all his property. You make him successful in whatever he does, and his flocks and herds are everywhere."

Even when Satan, that little lying devil, started attacking Job, he maintained his confidence in God even though he had lost all his children, all his livestock, and all his wealth. Read Job 1:13-20 (CEV) on your own.

Next, God allowed Satan to cover Job in boils from head to toe. Job 2:8-10 (CEV) says:

> Satan left and caused painful sores to break out all over Job's body—from head to toe. Then Job sat on the ash-heap to show his sorrow. And while he was scraping his sores with a broken piece of pottery, his wife asked, "Why do you still trust God? Why don't you curse him and die?" Job replied, "Don't talk like a fool! If we accept blessings from God, we must accept trouble as well." In all that happened, Job never once said anything against God.

Here we see Job's wife coming against him. Instead of seeking an answer from God, his wife sided with the little lying devil by telling Job to curse God and die. But Job still maintains his confidence in God. How many of us could handle a tragedy like Job's and come out in our right mind?

In 2001, my wife and I faced one of the hardest trials of our lives. During a time when we weren't working while trying to maintain two households, one in Lubbock and one in Hobbs, our eight-year-old boy was hit by a car. The accident shattered his face, broke his collarbone, snapped one of his legs in half, and put him in a coma for three weeks. I was in the waiting room with my older boy and my youngest daughter.

At least four doctors came to the waiting room and asked me to sign a form so they could operate on my son. I told them, "No, my God will heal him."

The woman doctor started talking to me really slowly and said, "Do you understand that your boy was in a major accident?"

I looked at her, confused. She got really close to me and said really slowly once again, "Do you comprehend what is going on with your boy?"

At this point, I was getting annoyed with her, so I spoke to her the same way she was speaking to me, really slowly, and I used my hands to demonstrate. I said, "My God in the heavens," as I pointed toward heaven, "is going to heal my son."

She looked so angry that I thought she was going to slap me. One of the other doctors pulled me to the side and said, "I am a Christian also, but we need to make a small cut to let the swelling expand."

As we talked, I saw that our conversations were going nowhere, so I said to the doctor, "Do you want to see a miracle?"

He said, "I have never seen one."

"My boy's face was shattered," I said, "and you will see my God heal it."

He replied, "If God does this miracle, I will give you an hour of my time to teach me about Him."

The team of doctors left, and my older boy said to me, "You know they were talking to you as if you were a retard."

I told him, "Don't hold it against them. They see things in the natural sense and don't understand the spiritual things of God."

That night about 4 a.m., I was meditating on God's Word as I was sitting and watching my son. As I watched him, I had so much joy within me even though our family had just been through a horrible tragedy. God causes our inner man to be full of glorious joy even when our lives are in complete turmoil.

At that moment, in the middle of the room, I saw a door open, and there was a light. I saw three people standing over my son, and they were performing surgery on him. One of the men turned toward me and smiled. I know it was a vision, but I felt as though I was in another dimension.

I felt the shekinah glory of the Lord in the room, God's divine presence. So, I dropped to my knees and started praising and thanking Him. At that moment, as I was in the presence of God, I knew He had healed my son. When I looked up toward the door where the light was coming from, the light just disappeared like a door shutting. I sat there with a glorious joy, and I pondered this experience with a smile on my face.

At 8 a.m. the doctor took my boy for x-rays and a CAT Scan to determine how he was going to repair all the shattered bones on my son's face. He came back to the room, however, to let me know that he didn't have to do anything because he couldn't find a broken bone on his face.

To God be all the Glory!

About an hour later, the neurosurgeon came in and said, "I have truly seen a miracle from God." With a concerned look, the doctor asked me why my boy was still in a coma. I told him if he woke up right now, he would feel all the pain from the swelling. God would never allow this, so when the swelling goes down, my boy will wake up. The doctor was true to his word; he set a date and let me teach him the Word of God.

Three weeks later, my boy woke up from a coma and didn't remember a thing about the accident. Six weeks later, while he was in rehab, our two older kids were involved in a car accident and died twenty minutes apart.

My wife and I have always done what Christ wanted us to do. But we didn't understand why all these tragedies were happening to us, especially so close together. All we could do was grab hold of the hand of God and not let go. I just had to tell my wife, "Don't focus on the dead. Look at our eight-year-old son and our three-year-old daughter. They are alive and need us right now."

God is with us in good times and in trials even when we don't understand the reasons for the trials. Our joy is not based on anything we are going through. It is based upon our relationship with Christ. God may use our current suffering to encourage others in the future. By choosing the right mindset, we can rise above our suffering and focus on the joy that comes from Christ.

Job had the mindset to trust God regardless of what was happening. Placing our trust in God brings joy. We have a God who lives in us and loves us more than we can ever imagine.

I praise and glorify the Lord of my salvation!

Chapter 34
Mercy and Compassion

Micah 6:8 (AMP) says, "And what does the Lord require of you. Except to be just, and to love [and to diligently practice] kindness (compassion), And to walk humbly with your God [setting aside any overblown sense of importance or self-righteousness]?"

We are to teach the things that Christ taught, not just in words, but also in our actions. To do the things that Christ did, that is to love, have mercy and compassion, be just, and to walk humbly with God. This is a spiritual formation being shaped in us by the Spirit of Christ. By doing the work He has given us to do, being instruments of righteousness as we submit our lives to Him.

I was flying out of Vera Cruz, Mexico, into Houston, Texas, and I had a short layover. There was a couple talking to each other about how they had been there for three days, and the airlines kept saying the same thing day after day that they would be boarding soon. They had no money.

Then God gave me a great compassion for them, so I gave them three hundred dollars.

I walked away because my flight was boarding. As I was waiting to board my flight, his wife came crying and thanked me. She hugged me and was still crying. My spirit was in agony that I felt such a great compassion for her, that I pulled out all the money I had in my pocket and gave it to her. She said, "I'm not asking for more," and I looked toward her and said, "That's all I have; I don't have anymore."

She thought I was talking to her, but I was talking to the Lord. He was telling me to give all I have. I emptied my pockets and gave her another five hundred dollars. I can only imagine what they thought, *Is he an angel helping us?*

There was another lady that came and bought a poodle puppy from me. She loved that dog just like she loved her kids. Several months later she called wanting to know if I had any puppies. I didn't have any puppies for sale, but I had one that was about four months old that I was keeping back for myself.

She explained to me that the neighbor next door had a daughter about fifteen years old that has a poodle about three years old, and she was always playing with her dog. The dog was her life to her in a sense. She said the dog got run over by a car and died. The young lady was hysterical and crying like she had just lost a child. I could only imagine the agony she was going through.

I felt a compassion come over me for the young lady even though I did not know her. The lady lived about an hour from me, and I told her, "If you come and pick up the puppy, I will give the young lady the dog at no charge." She came and brought the young lady with her to pick up her new puppy.

God treats us with compassion, and He wants us to give compassion to a hurting world. There is a scripture that I enjoy, and I wish people would follow it: 1 John 3:18 (TLB), "Little children, let us stop just saying we love people; let us really love them, and show it by our actions."

I praise and glorify the Lord!

Chapter 35
Being Obedient When God Calls You

In 2021, I was in prayer, and the Lord spoke to me in my spirit. He brought Mike to my mind and said, "Go see Mike." When God tells me to go, I don't question it; I just do it. I didn't know Mike that well on a personal level, but I knew him on a spiritual level. He has always had the love, peace, and joy of God in him. Matthew 7:20 (NKJV) says, "Therefore by their fruits you will know them."

I went to his place of business and said to him, "God sent me here, so what is going on?"

He gave me a strange look at first, and then he said, "My boy is in a coma and they have him on life support."

I asked him, "Where do they have him?"

And he said, "Lubbock, Texas."

I told him, "Tomorrow I will go and see him in Lubbock. And whatever God shows me, I will let you know." When

God is calling you to pray for someone, more than likely He is going to do something big.

The following day I went to the hospital and saw Mike and his wife. They took me to the room where their son was. His entire body was swollen. As I was looking at him, the Lord didn't show me death; He showed me life. I turned to Mike and said, "Your boy isn't going to die. I don't see death; I see life in him." And then I prayed for him and left.

The five senses, hearing, smelling, seeing, touching, and tasting, are also in the spiritual world. Mike had to choose to believe the Word of God in the spiritual sense for healing or to believe what the doctors were telling him with their natural senses. Instead of listening to Satan and looking at our situation, we must be working together with God who heals us by His Word. The prayer of agreement is powerful when used the right way.

We need to get all our friends and relatives to agree with us and make a positive confession for our healing. Faith is having complete trust and confidence in God, knowing we can depend upon Him to do what He says He will do. As I turned to Mike and gave him God's Word, that is, "Your boy isn't going to die; I see life in him," he sighed in relief. His spirit was accepting the Word of God and running with it. I didn't see Mike for a long time after that day.

The Bible recounts the stories of some Godly men in bad situations. Jonah comes to mind. Jonah 2:8-9 (KJV) says, "They that observe lying vanities forsake their own mercy. But I will sacrifice unto thee with the voice of thanksgiving; I will pay that that I have vowed. Salvation is of the Lord."

While Jonah was in the belly of the whale, he started praying for mercy because he knew that God is a loving, merciful, and compassionate God who loves His children and would do anything for them. So he didn't lose faith in God.

There is no visible proof that God answered his prayer. Jonah's symptoms inside the whale were very real. While he didn't deny them, he called them "lying vanities." Jonah was looking toward the promises of God and not at the situation he was facing.

Faced with the same situation, most of us would lose hope in God. But Jonah said, "They that observe lying vanities forsake their own mercy." Jonah had a complete understanding of God's Word and confidence in the Lord. He offered continual praises to Him.

Imagine yourself in the water with the stench of dead fish and seaweed all around you. There is no way to get a whiff of fresh air, and you cannot get the dead smell out of your nose. I don't know about you, but I can't imagine myself in this mess; it's too hard.

Now think about God's promises and His divine mercy for you.

Now start singing, praising, and thanking God for the situation you're in, just like Jonah did.

Now you have a choice: you can either observe the problem, or you can observe the answer. Remember what Jonah said, "If I observe the problem, I am going to forsake my own mercy."

A lot of us have been watching our situations, the symptoms, the pain, and the bad reports in the natural, and we wonder why God's mercy doesn't show up! Hebrews 13:15

(KJV) says, "By him therefore let us offer the sacrifice of praise to God continually, that is, the fruit of our lips giving thanks to his name." The Holy Spirit commands us to praise and thank Him continually. We aren't supposed to be occupied with what we see or feel in the natural, as doing so would violate the faith and turn off the switch to God's power.

Returning to Mike's story, after a few years I was in a Bible study and Mike gave his testimony about his son. He said, "Remember when you came to the hospital to pray for my son? My wife and I were in the room when the doctor walked in and gave us the bad news. He said, 'Your son hasn't responded to any of our treatments, so we are going to take him off life support and let him die.'

The doctor had just walked out of the room when you walked in and said, 'Take me to your son.' You saw my son and then turned toward me and said that you didn't see death; you saw life in him. Then you prayed for him and walked away. Let me tell you what happened after that.

After they took my son off life support, he didn't die. The following two weeks, the doctors were making calls to other hospitals to see if they had ever seen anything like this. God had His hand on my boy, and everything the doctors were taught by medical science wasn't lining up with what they were seeing.

As soon as the swelling came down, my boy woke up, and he recovered from his sickness. To God be all the glory!"

All these testimonies happened because I was obedient to God when He called me to go.

To God be all the Glory!

Made in the USA
Middletown, DE
16 July 2024